MODERN DAY HEA

CW01668292

Miracles in the Bible, Chu

"My Lord, I believe that you are the God of Miracles and that you have created me to see every challenge and every problem *I face as an opportunity for a miracle that you are ready, willing, and about to perform."*

Selva Sugunendran

CEng, MIEE, MCMI, CHt, MIMDHA, MBBNLP, MGONLP
#1 Best Selling Author, Speaker & Coach

ISBN: *978-163625854-6*

Medical Disclaimer: The author of this book is a competent, experienced writer. He has taken every opportunity to ensure that all information presented here is correct and up to date at the time of writing. No documentation within this book has been evaluated by the Food and Drug Administration, and no documentation should be used to diagnose, treat, cure, or prevent any disease.

Any information is to be used for educational and information purposes only. It should never be substituted for medical advice from your doctor or other health care professionals.

We do not dispense medical advice, prescribe drugs, or diagnose any illnesses with our literature.

The author and publisher are not responsible or liable for any self or third-party diagnosis made by visitors based upon the content of this book. The author or publisher does not in any way endorse any commercial products or services linked from other websites to this book.

Please, always consult your doctor or health care specialist if you are in any way concerned about your physical wellbeing.

DEDICATION

This Book Is Dedicated to All Those Who Desire Miracles in their lives just as they were "normal" when Christ was on Earth

Lord, I pray for the person reading this book. Father Lord work powerfully in their lives. May they receive the healing miracles they believe you for, and in the same measure use them to heal others. Bring about the miracles you have promised us at all times, especially in modern times. Let your Kingdom, the one where there is no pain or sickness; come into their lives right now. Pour out your Holy Spirit's power to heal and to save them. In Jesus' mighty name, I pray, Amen.

Table of Contents

PART IV

PART V

FOREWORD

Different people have come up with varying reasons as to why they believe healing only happened in Bible times even though Scriptures say otherwise. This book seeks to help you understand that healing is part of the atonement, just like salvation, and it is for us today as much as it was for people in the Bible times.

After the author discovered that some people believe healing miracles were not for today, he spent some time seeking God about this and then did extensive research on the topic. The author uses the 7 key facts he was given by God and scriptural truths to show how miracles have been happening since the story of creation up to today.

Understand that you need to know and believe that God wants you well, and he is still in the healing business for you to be able to fight for your healing from the point of victory.

The author starts the first part of this book by showing you why miracles matter in the world today. You will get to see and understand the importance of miracles and see different examples of miracles that took place in the Old Testament and the New Testament.

You will also read about the different miracles that have happened in the modern world and why you should expect your miracles today. You will understand why some people do not get healed despite healing being part of the atonement.

In the second part of the book, you will find out why positive affirmations are important for people who are trusting God for healing miracles and abundant life. You will learn how to create your own Christian affirmations. The author has gone ahead and created affirmations that you can start using right away.

Part three of the book is intended to show readers that modern-day healing is real, and there are people around the world who have experienced healing miracles in their lives and the lives of their loved ones. The reader will get to read different testimonies of how God came through and healed people from different parts of the world. The author has included poems in the fourth part of the book to encourage and inspire readers.

By the time you finish reading the content in this book, you will be inspired, your faith for healing will be stirred up, and you will no longer live in defeat.

May the blessings of the Lord and his healing power rest upon you!

Susie Ward

VERY IMPORTANT MESSAGE FROM THE AUTHOR

Before you dive into the first chapter of this book, please read this message because it is very important.......

Soon after I learned that my last book titled, "Empowering Healing & Hope Through Faith" had become a #1 Best Seller three times around the world within 21 days, I started talking to several people who read the book. I was so happy to hear them say how blessed they were after reading the book.

Soon I started asking them whether they had shared the information in the book with others. It became clear that though the people who read the book were blessed by the message, some of their friends, including church members, felt that the miracles that were "normal" when Christ was on earth don't happen as much in the modern world.

I spent the next 2 weeks after this revelation examining why people felt that way. One evening, before going to bed, I prayed to God to give me guidance on how I could help those who believe miracles only happened in the past; they are not for modern times. At around 3am, I woke up and felt very excited, and the words that came to me were, "How you should see Miracles".

I quickly reached for my notepad and pen and started writing down the thoughts that came to me. By the time I was done writing, I had 7 bullet points.

I have expanded on the 7 points, and may I suggest that you read through these points below at least once before you start reading the rest of the book, which is based on the 7 points.

God Bless.
Selva

HOW YOU SHOULD SEE MIRACLES

The dictionary defines a miracle as an extraordinary event or achievement that is not explicable by natural or scientific laws and is therefore attributed to a supernatural being. Despite this definition, it has still been a quest by many to find out whether or not these happenings that are beyond human explanation, do take place.

Some say humans might not have evolved to the point of understanding why things happen the way they do. For others, science may be just as limiting as the researchers' minds. Then some shun the fact that it is above human understanding and accuse the views of others on the same. In their argument, they state that 6 can be seen as 9 with respect to the viewer's position. But my question is, why not look from the viewer's perspective? Below are a few points on how you should see miracles:

1. **There is absolutely NO reason why Miracles in the Modern Day shouldn't be as normal as when Jesus Christ was on earth 2000 years ago—Christ performed miracles wherever He went.**

Let me start with ignition to activate logical thinking and analysis of what we see around us daily. To date, no valid explanations have been given to prove what surrounds the formation of a cell, the smallest unit of life, much less about the conception and birth of a human being. This should, therefore, be the prime reason behind the belief in miracles, which dates not only 2000 years after Christ but stand tall since the beginning of creation.

The fact that the creation of the cell and human being has remained a gem buried far away from the miner's pickaxe paves an underlying acknowledgment that modern-day miracles are not different from those that happened when Christ was on earth. According to the Holy Scriptures, Christ fed thousands of people with just five loaves of bread and two fishes. He made the lame to walk and gave back life to the dead 2000 years ago. Today we still see people being fed without known sources of food; people still get healed from deadly infirmities; others resuscitate from death after long periods of complete loss of vital signs, all without logical or medical explanations.

The problem is some people expect miracles to be the exact same as one plus one equals two. Similar miracles indeed happen today, but different miracles than just the feeding of a multitude, the healing of the lame, and raising of the dead also occur around the world. Christ promised to send the Holy Spirit after ascending to heaven – which he did. This Holy Spirit, who is *In Persona Christi* – one with Christ, remains alive and active not only where Christ lived and performed miracles but in omnipresence.

2. You should see God as the source of miracles

Most of us enjoy snowboarding without thinking where the snow comes from or how it is formed. Or we enjoy the sumptuousness of a pizza without necessarily giving a thought of how its ingredients came about. Like the fruit of a given tree, the essence accumulated in it reflects precisely what the tree is made of. A fruit cannot contain what its tree does not have neither can it give the fruit what it lacks. The same thing applies to miracles and their source.

You have probably heard this famous saying a couple of times, *"seeing is believing".* If we intend to see miracles without seeing God as the source, it will be as though we are talking about snow without thinking of water – which is the source of the snow itself. As we mentioned in point **1**above, the creation of the world is a miracle, so is the creator Himself. According to the Holy Book, in the beginning, God said, 'Let there be light, and there was and let the waters gather, and it so happened.' If these and more happened within the twinkle of an eye, I guess failure to see God as a miracle is more than failing to see the human being as the result of a miracle itself.

3. You should believe in the God of miracles

We make plans for the following day before going to bed every night and wake up to realize them or review our schedule for others. Rarely do we even think that we may not wake up or that we may not realize what we planned the previous day. We go to bed believing that we are going to wake to a new day and execute our projects, period. The same thing applies to how a child giggles whenever we throw it into the air. It believes that we can't let it fall. A baby trusts the capability of the parent or loved one.

If a child believes in a mere human (who is not its creator), how much should we believe in the God of miracles - our creator? It seems as though we are skeptical about acknowledging the presence and works of God and thus failing to see the miracles happening in our midst on a day to day basis. Miracles happen where and when they are least expected. The more we believe in the God of miracles, the clearer we see His works.

4. **You should be convinced that your life is made for miracles**

If we are to step into a forger's workshop right now, we will notice the tools he has adapted to suit his quest. These tools may not be the same for every forger, but they are always distinct and made to fulfill the purpose for which they are created. It will, therefore, not be erroneous to say that human beings are like tools at the service of their creator.

A similar situation is seen when cartoonists create characters and make them play in well-determined parts of a movie. It is the same way God uses each and every one of us as a tool to realize His miracles. As mentioned earlier, man is a miracle, and we should, therefore, be mindful of the fact that only a miracle can be made to realize another. In other words, only a lighted candle can light another.

5. **Stop looking at symptoms & circumstances that cause concern, pain, or suffering.**

When moving on the streets, we sometimes tend to bypass some people or objects without noticing - not because they are out of our scope of vision but because we are focused on things or objectives, we deem more important. Let us call this; Selective Seeing. We should, therefore, choose to look see the positive side of things and not the pain or negativity in them. When we tell our minds our top priority, our eyes focus on the set objectives, no matter where we find ourselves.

The Holy Bible tells us in *John 16:21, "A woman is in pain because her hour has come, but when her child is born, she no longer remembers the anguish because of the joy of having brought a human being into the world."* This is a reminder that whenever we face pain or trouble, we should look at the joy hidden behind it. We do more than digging through hard rocks of the earth's crust to harness oil beneath so that we can use it as fuel to light a lamp and chase the night. Meanwhile, uncovering the marvels – the miracles of God does not require as much pain and effort.

6. See all problems as opportunities for imminent miracles.

When a medical practitioner is undergoing training, he takes an interest in sickness and even death of humans and animals as well, to draw knowledge and exercise his job with better precision in the future. The greater the diversity of diseases and disorders he comes across, the more he gets armed. We equally notice that an athlete will prefer training on steep terrain in order to compete on a less difficult one. This way, he gives himself added advantage over his peers because he might have encountered most of the difficulties found on the competition ground.

We need to look at the problems we encounter on a day to day basis the same way medical students and athletes do. We need to see them as opportunities for imminent miracles. As they say, God hides behind ordinary things to do extraordinary works. All we need to do is to see every difficulty as a gateway to a miracle, thus acknowledging the hand of God in it.

7. **Believe and say to yourself every day, "My Lord, I believe that you are the God of Miracles and that you have created me to see every challenge and every problem I face as an opportunity for a miracle that you are ready, willing and about to perform in my life."**

If only man had faith as small as a mustard seed, he would command the mountains to move, and they would move. *In Proverbs 18:21, we read that "Death and life are in the power of the tongue, and those who love it will eat its fruits."* These words from the Holy Book tell us more about the power of the tongue in particular and belief in general. An African saying goes like this: "*The hand which opens to give is obviously open to receive."* This is to say that when we open our hearts and minds for God's will to be done in us, we do not go empty without harnessing the miraculous benefits that come with it. If we prophesy and call on God to be with us, His abundant love will flow in us. We should be able to believe in miracles and the fact that God is the author of all that we see and have. Life in itself is a miracle.

Think about the conception of a fetus and how it feeds and grows in us. Science will explain several things regarding this. It tells us about the way the sperm cell fuses with the egg and after which life begins. Let's take a second to ask ourselves how the sperm cell comes about, to start with, and when we get thinking, we see God's miracle one on one. Miracles are around us every day; Waking up, having food to eat, going to bed...pretty much in everything we do because we cannot guarantee that the next minute is a certainty.

In conclusion, I would like to emphasize that miracles take place as many times as we breathe and we just need to look in God's direction, and the power of the Holy Spirit will guide us to see more.

Each and every one of us should choose whether or not to live this earthly journey buried in darkness or walk in the light of His miracles. However, before making your choice on the path to take, it is essential to keep in mind that it is simply awesome and glorious when you chose to rely on Him for all, knowing that he will always miraculously handle all our burdens the right way. It might not be the way we expect but trust that it will ALWAYS be the best for us.

INTRODUCTION

And awe came upon every soul, and many wonders and signs were being done through the apostles (Acts 2:43, ESV).

Joe was a pastor of a young church plant in its fifth year of existence. The congregation was made up mostly of jobless college students and always seemed to be on the edge of financial collapse. Beginning the second year, each December, the congregation took up a Christmas offering. Most of the time, the offering was used to make up for budget shortfalls. The church was generous, but again, it was also quite poor.

That said, they always seemed to come through. On average, the offering would amount to $5000, which was just enough. But in the fifth year, the leadership of the church decided to do things differently. They asked for a special offering that was higher than the usual amount of $5000. Call it risk-taking, inexperience, and a little foolishness, or faith, either way, they needed a miracle. As the day for the Christmas offering approached, the members prayed to God that he would not only provide but that he would provide *through the members.* They didn't want the provision to come through some outside windfall but from their own faithfulness. But could you get blood from a turnip? Did they even have the resources to give? They prayed and waited, anyway.

Two weeks before the church was to take up the offering, the pastor, Joe, had a dream. In the dream, he was standing in front of a slot machine. He pulled the arm of the machine and hit the jackpot. What came out was thirty thousand dollars. When Joe woke up, he immediately had the thought, "What if God is telling me that our Christmas offering, which had never exceeded $5000, was going to be $30,000?" This seemed incredible and unlikely. But still, Joe shared the dream with the bookkeeper and the staff and asked them to pray for $30,000. Everyone was skeptical but willing.

Finally, the day arrived. No one but the staff was aware of the dream. The church members were counseled to obey God and give whatever had impressed in their hearts. When they counted the money after the service, the total added up to $29,993. The bookkeeper, who had been aware of the dream and the prayers, opened his wallet and threw in the extra $7. The result was not only God's provision, but an astounding measure of faith added to the small but growing congregation, who worshipped mightily when they were told about the miracle.

It would be tempting to call the large amount of money the miracle, but in truth, it was merely radical faithfulness from generous lovers of God. But the dream could have no other label. God miraculously revealed the amount of money to pray for, and though only a few people were aware of the dream, the congregation was moved by God to give.

Why Do Miracles Matter?

The first answer to this question is that miracles matter to God, so they should matter to us. But what exactly is a miracle? A woman will find her keys after losing them for three days and call it a miracle. A man may get a passing grade on a test that he was sure he failed and call it a miracle. But is it?

Dictionary.com defines miracles as:

- an effect or extraordinary event in the physical world that surpasses all known human or natural powers and is ascribed to a supernatural cause.
- such an effect or event manifesting or considered as a work of God.
- a wonder; marvel.
- a wonderful or surpassing example of some quality

For the purposes of this book, we shall go with the first three definitions. Many who choose not to believe in God will do so by saying that miracles are impossible, they cannot be true, so the Bible and God cannot be accurate. But that is not true, at least according to the definition of a miracle.

In some ways, it is right to call miracles the natural wonders of creation. Consider the conception and growth of a baby in a womb. People commonly refer to that as "the miracle of childbirth." Or consider the infinitely delicate task of creating a universe that works in perfect harmony, such as this planet that we call home. It is a miracle that the oxygen level remains stable for life and that the gravitational pull is perfectly calibrated.

But Biblical miracles are something different altogether. God designed the laws of nature and physical reality. It seems evident from Scriptural accounts, historical records, and personal anecdotes that one reason he designed the natural laws was to break them at will to show his power and to bring glory to his name while blessing his people. This book is a brief study of the miraculous with an emphasis on how to think about and pray for miracles today. My assertion is that miracles exist today, just like they did in the past. Miracles serve the exact purposes they did in bible times: to give glory to God and bless his people.

CHAPTER 1

THE KINGDOM OF GOD AND THE GLORY OF GOD

In my previous book, ***Empowering Healing & Hope Through Faith***, I said that Jesus' healing ministry was his way of demonstrating the kingdom of God. Healing is under one category with miracle-working. So we can say that by performing miracles, Jesus authoritatively proclaimed the kingdom of God.

A lot has been and will be said about miracles. But the truth is God still performs miracles, and they always serve a purpose. To see a miracle, you need to trust God and believe that the miracles we read in Scripture truly happened. Witnessing the manifestation of miracles is always a tremendous blessing and should cause us to glorify God. It should also deepen our faith.

When Jesus was born, his birth was shrouded in miracles. Visitations by angels, prophetic words, and heavenly choruses surrounded the greatest miracle of all, the Virgin birth of God the Son come to save. He lived a relatively normal life as the adopted son of a carpenter, Joseph, who taught him his trade. Then, when Jesus was around thirty years old, this happened:

And he came to Nazareth, where he had been brought up. And as was his custom, he went to the synagogue on the Sabbath day, and he stood up to read. And the scroll of the prophet Isaiah was given to him. He unrolled the scroll and found the place where it was written,

"The Spirit of the Lord is upon me because he has anointed me to proclaim good news to the poor. He has sent me to proclaim liberty to the captives and recovering of sight to the blind, to set at liberty those who are oppressed, to proclaim the year of the Lord's favour." And he rolled up the scroll and gave it back to the attendant and sat down. And the eyes of all in the synagogue were fixed on him. And he began to say to them, "Today this Scripture has been fulfilled in your hearing" (Luke 4:16-21, ESV).

To summarize, Jesus went into the synagogue and read from Isaiah, who said that God would visit his people to save them at the appointed time. The signs would be miracles and the preaching of good news. Then Jesus said in verse 21 that the time had come for that particular Scripture to be fulfilled. He implied and later proved that *he* was the fulfillment. How did he prove it?

Through miracles. Immediately after this, we see the clear pattern of demonstration of the kingdom of God having partially come, and the proclamation of that kingdom and himself as the king. Later he would say,

If I am not doing the works of my Father, then do not believe me; but if I do them, even though you do not believe me, believe the works, that you may know and understand that the Father is in me and I am in the Father (Jn 10:37-38, ESV).

And then, "Believe me that I am in the Father and the Father is in me, or else believe on account of the works themselves" (Jn 14:11, ESV).

When God gives signs and wonders, it is for the sake of helping his people to believe in him, to show his power, and glorify himself.

God Does Everything for His Own Glory

The idea of God doing everything, including miracles for his own glory, doesn't sit well with some people. But why is that? It is because they look at this from a humanistic point of view. For them, it is hard to understand why God needs all the glory because they look at God the same way they look at themselves. These people know that they fall short all the time, and therefore they will never be worthy of any glory. But they forget that they are human and God is well... God! He is perfect and deserves all the glory, so it is okay for him to glorify himself.

Our universe-- the seen and the unseen heavenly dimension-- works properly when it is in the right order. God is at the top of it all, having created it all, and he deserves all the glory.

Understand this, with or without our acknowledgment and praise, God is still amazingly glorious. Praising God is for our own good more than it is for his sake. If we don't glorify God and praise Him, we shall live unfulfilling lives. When we don't allow God to take his rightful place in our lives, we end up having the wrong assumptions about the universe. We become dishonest or at least live in error, and we get tempted to see everything else wrongly.

The worst error men make to worship themselves, giving themselves the highest place. When God shows his power through the natural or miraculous, it is out of his great mercy towards men and women. Nothing will take us down like pride, and nothing will build us up like praising, worshiping, and glorifying the most glorious and praiseworthy One in existence. To witness a miracle is a tremendous blessing for this reason.

So the two reasons for miracles are to demonstrate the existence of God to a people who are hungry for him as a sign of the reality of his kingdom. And to display his power so that men and women can give Him glory and stay in a right relationship with God and with creation.

In the next chapter, we will explore the Old Testament to see how God did exactly this, including what he said about the matter.

CHAPTER 2

MIRACLES AND THE POWER OF GOD IN GENESIS

There was nothing, and out of nothing came everything. This was the first and perhaps the greatest miracle of all. Maybe you were like me as a child, wondering where God lived before he created heaven, wondering where he put the universe when he created it, and where he came from. Now that we are grown, we know better and understand that these questions are not answerable.

What we do know is that there was nothing. No- thing. Except for one God in three persons. At some point, he spoke heaven and heavenly creatures into being, and then one day, God said, "Let there *be*." A miracle of creation. Men and women create, but none of us has created out of nothing. It is only God that has done that.

In the beginning, was the Word, and the Word was with God, and the Word was God. He was in the beginning with God. All things were made through him, and without him was not anything made that was made (Jn 1:1-3, ESV).

A Christian doesn't need to believe in a literal six-day creation of all things, but *why not?* What do you see in this God that would stop you from believing that he cannot create a universe in one moment, let alone six days? Again, there is a great mystery here, but our primary response should be awe, thanksgiving, and worship.

A walk through the Old Testament will reveal a God who is often content to let nature take its course, but who always intervenes at the right time to accomplish his purposes.

Genesis

After the miracle of creation, God makes man in his image.

In Genesis 2, we get to see another angle on his creation, particularly of man and woman. God created the man and called him Adam. After showing Adam that no suitable helper could be found for him among the animals Adam lived within the garden, he caused him to fall into a deep sleep and removed one of Adam's ribs. This was a miracle. Even before man invented anesthetic, Adam was put under one by God for surgery, and then the rib was removed in some miraculous way.

But imagine what it looked like for the woman to spring out of that one bone. Miraculous! And Adam certainly seemed to know how to appreciate a miracle when he saw one:

Then the man said, "This, at last, is bone of my bones and flesh of my flesh;

she shall be called Woman, because she was taken out of Man" (Gen 2:23, ESV).

After this, the tragedy of the serpent and the forbidden fruit happened, and man obtained the knowledge of good and evil. They knew that they were naked and were cast out of paradise. The greatest miracle of all was already in motion; God would one day send his Son, the lamb of God, slain since the foundation of the world, but for now, the story of God and his people would play out for millennia. Nature would take its course, and God would allow the man to rule in his image. Occasionally God would intervene, but for the most part, even Satan and demons were allowed to have their way.

It is incredible how God sovereignly rules the universe through created beings that he has given free will. Human history is mysterious, and different cultures have left us many clues as to the nature of the divine intervention, but what we know for sure is what the Bible tells us. Aside from the miracle of God condescending to speak to men (such as with Cain and Noah), the next miracle happens in Genesis 11. If you are wondering about the flood and Noah's ark, consider the facts. God told Noah to build an ark, which he did for 120 years. It would have been miraculous if the ark had merely appeared. The rains flooded the earth, which obviously shows God's power, but God is always the one who makes it rain. This is still God behind the *natural* working of the world. Some say there was no rain in those days up to that time, but it is not clear from Scripture that that is the case.

The people of the earth built the great tower at Babel, a great city built by Nimrod, a mighty hunter in the Lord (Gen 10:9), and God "came down" to see it. There was something about it that God considered to be disobedience. Likely, it represented their desire to trust in themselves and not God, and their unwillingness to do what he asked that is spread over the face of the earth. The miracle that happened was that God gave them many different languages. He created a sort of tribalism that would cause them to scatter all over the world.

Part of God's plan from chapter one was that humans would multiply over the face of the earth. We don't quite know it by Genesis 11, but he wanted people to populate the earth and form different nations. Why? That is for him to know, and we can only offer some good guesses. But *that* he wanted it is clear. So, just like that, men and women spoke different languages and went off together to find new cities, and eventually, new countries.

Another great story that is full of miracles is the story of Abram, who was later renamed, Abraham. God told him to leave his home country and sent him with his wife and his nephew Lot into Canaan by way of Egypt. After Abraham's foolish decision to allow the Egyptian Pharaoh to have his wife, God "afflicted Pharaoh and his household with great plagues" (Gen 12:17, ESV).

Abraham made a blood covenant with God by the ritual of the torch and the fire pot (Gen 15;9-21). He saw angels come down to rescue Lot from Sodom and the destruction of that wicked place by fire from heaven. Lot's wife turned to salt; Sarah, though barren and very old, gave birth to Isaac. Before that, Abraham gave her away to another king, who also experienced the wrath of God; Abraham then prayed for the man and his household, and the women were healed of barrenness. You might also say that the ram in the thicket when God tested Abraham's faith by asking him to sacrifice his only son, a foreshadow of the sacrifice of God's own Son for the sins of the world, was a miracle. The last miracle in the life of Abraham was concerning his servant's mission to find a wife for Isaac. God answered the servant's prayer and sent him to the one who was to be Isaac's wife.

Later in Genesis, there is the story of Jacob's dream of the ladder and his conversation with God (Gen 28:10-17). Later on, he increases the size of his flocks with a strange trick that can only be attributed to the intervention of God (Gen 30). On the way back home with his large family and great wealth, he wrestles with God (Gen 32:22-32).

Then there is the story of Joseph, the dreamer, and the dream interpreter. God shows him what will happen in Egypt, and Joseph, who had been sold into slavery, rises to the top as the right arm of Pharaoh. It would take many books to discuss all the miracles God performed in the history of man in the Old Testament. We can only mention a few great miracles he performed here.

Reading through Genesis, it is incredible how there are a few instances of God's intervention through miracles. But he came through when they were necessary. All these give us an idea of what the people of God are to be all about when God is not doing miracles, which is allowing us to continue bearing his image to the world and accomplishing his purposes in the mundane of day-to-day life. We should pray for miracles, but we should not think that God is absent when he lets things play out naturally, for that seems to be his preferred method.

CHAPTER 3

MIRACLES AND THE POWER OF GOD IN THE REST OF THE OLD TESTAMENT

In the last chapter, we looked at Genesis and saw that God rarely intervened in the creation, but when he did, it was to accomplish his primary purpose of creation and the redemption of that creation that had fallen. In this chapter, we will look at the rest of the Old Testament in regards to his work of the miraculous, and see if there is a pattern and what we can learn from the stories.

Exodus

While it was God's providential hand that caused Moses to survive the infanticide of Pharaoh in his day-- floating in a basket in the Nile, avoiding predators, and finding refuge in the arms of Pharaoh's daughter-- it wasn't quite what you would call a miracle. The miracle happened eighty years later when the same baby found himself tending sheep in the wilderness. Having lost one of them, he had gone looking for it and stumbled onto holy ground. There he witnessed a miracle.

There was a bush that was on fire but was not being consumed. This was a miracle. It defied natural law about what should happen when fire meets wood. This certainly got Moses' attention so that he paid attention when the next miracle occurred. The bush spoke.

More accurately, God spoke. "Take off your shoes. You stand on holy ground!" Moses obeyed and witnessed many more miracles as God called him to go back to Egypt (from where he had fled as a murderer when he was forty) and demand that Pharaoh let his people go from their bondage and slavery. Moses, said God, would be a great miracle worker, and by these miracles, God would smite the Egyptians and their demonic gods.

What ultimately made Moses bold enough to undertake this task? The miracles that he witnessed, along with the miracle of the audible voice of God. Why did God favour Moses so much as to show him these miracles? Because he knew that Moses needed a sign. What God asked would be impossible without supernatural intervention. He was asking Moses to raise an army and rebel. God was promising to do all the work.

Moses obeyed, and accompanied by his long-lost brother Aaron, he performed miracle after miracle for Pharaoh and his magicians whose dark arts were also impressive but no match for Moses and his God. After the plague miracles and the great Passover miracle, Pharaoh let them go. Only to be the victim of one last miracle when

God parted the Red Sea for his people to walk safely through, and then closed it on Pharaoh's army, drowning most of them.

In the wilderness, the miracles were God's provision: manna and quail from heaven, and water from rocks. For forty years, and still, at the end of those years, God regularly showed his power as he provided and protected his people.

Joshua

After Moses died and gave the mantle of leadership to Joshua, including the power of God for miracles, the Israelites continued to see God work in the Promised Land. God's first priority was to confer Moses' authority onto Joshua by granting another miracle of parting the waters. The Israelites crossed the Jordan with the Ark of the Covenant, and all the people walked through it. In Joshua 3:7-13, God told them exactly why he was performing this miracle:

And the Lord said to Joshua, "Today I will begin to exalt you in the eyes of all Israel, so they may know that I am with you as I was with Moses. Tell the priests who carry the Ark of the Covenant: 'When you reach the edge of the Jordan's waters, go and stand in the river.'"

Joshua said to the Israelites, "Come here and listen to the words of the Lord your God. This is how you will know that the living God is among you and that he will certainly drive out before you the Canaanites, Hittites, Hivites, Perizzites, Girgashites, Amorites, and Jebusites. See, the Ark of the Covenant of the Lord of all the earth will go into the Jordan ahead of you. Now then, choose twelve men from the tribes of Israel, one from each tribe. And as soon as the priests who carry the ark of the Lord—the Lord of all the earth—set foot in the Jordan, its waters flowing downstream will be cut off and stand up in a heap (NIV)."

"Today, I will begin to exalt you in the eyes of all Israel, so they know I am with you as I was with Moses." God simply wanted to exalt Joshua so that people would listen to him. God wanted to accomplish his purposes through Joshua, but he needed to elevate his authority to do it. And then Joshua says in verse 10, *"This is how you will know that the living God is among you and that he will certainly drive out before you the Canaanites, Hittites, Hivites, Perizzites, Girgashites, Amorites and Jebusites."* The other purpose of the miracle was to give the Israelites faith that they would be able to drive out the people in the Promised Land as long as the miracle-working God was on their side.

There were many more times that God intervened on behalf of the Israelites in this period, but most notable was the defeat of Jericho when God caused the walls to crumble as the Israelites performed a ritual of walking around the city, blowing a trumpet and shouting.

Judges

After the death of Joshua, God raised up a succession of judges to lead his people. The Israelites remained a stubborn people throughout this time. God would send a judge to help them. They would succeed for a while, but then they would succumb to the temptation to worship the idols of the Canaanites. God would leave them for a time, and they would finally cry out to him, repenting and asking for help. He would call a judge, put his Spirit on him, and he would deliver them. But the first real miracles we see are in the days of Gideon when the Israelites are oppressed again, this time by the Midianites.

Gideon was not a man of great stature. God often uses such men to display his power and glory. First, Gideon was called by an angel. Second, the angel confirmed the call of Gideon by performing miracles. The first was by consuming with one touch the sacrifice prepared by Gideon for God, and the second was the famous fleece miracle (Ju 6:36-40). Gideon wanted proof that God was really going to do what he said, so he asked God to make the fleece he had set on the ground to be covered in dew while the rest of the ground was dry. If that wasn't enough, the next night, he asked for the opposite. In both cases, God proved himself through this sign. Gideon was on the hook.

God continued to intervene on behalf of the Israelites in the Book of Judges, but the next real miracles came through Samson. First was the miracle of his great strength. He simply could not be defeated, and he routinely fought off armies of Philistines. Ultimately, because of his foolishness, he trusted a woman who meant him harm and cut his hair, causing the vow between Samson and God to be nullified for a time. Samson was captured, and his eyes were gouged out. His last miracle occurred when he was brought out to be displayed to the Philistines in a large hall held up by mighty beams. Samson prayed to God one last time and pulled the hall down on himself and 3000 Philistines. God's purpose was to bring judgment on the Philistines through this miracle.

Samuel, Kings, and Chronicles

The size and scope of this book does not allow for a detailed chronicle of all the times that God miraculously intervened in the Old Testament. A brief list to end this section will have to suffice:

- The gift of a child to the barren Hannah who would give her son, Samuel, to the Lord (1 Sam 1)
- The voice of the Lord to Samuel (1 Sam 3)
- The curses on the Philistines and their god Dagon for capturing and holding the Ark of the covenant (1 Sam 5-6)
- Countless prophetic words
- The Spirit of the Lord upon Saul (1 Sam 10)
- Miraculous thunder and rain (1 Sam 12)
- Jonathan's miraculous defeat of the Philistines with his armor-bearer (1 Sam 14)
- The anointing of David (1 Sam 16)
- David's defeat of the giant, Goliath (1 Sam 17)
- David's miraculous prowess in battle
- The power of the Mighty Men of David in battle
- Solomon's prayer for wisdom (1 Kg 3)

- The Lord's presence in the Temple (1 Kg 8)
- The Lord's appearance to Solomon (1 Kg 9)
- Countless prophecies (1 Kg - Malachi)
- Elijah's drought (1 Kg 17)
- Elijah's flour and oil for the widow (1 Kg 17)
- Elijah raises the widow's son (1 Kg 17)
- Elijah defeats the Baal prophets (1 Kg 18)
- Elijah fed at the brook (1 Kg 19)
- Call of Elisha (1 Kg 19)
- Fire consumes the men who came to take Elijah (2 Kg 1)
- Elijah taken to heaven (2 Kg 2)
- She-bears consume the youths who jeered at Elisha (2 Kg 2)
- Elisha's perpetual oil for the widow (2 Kg 4)
- The miraculous birth of the Shunammite's son by word of Elisha (2 Kg 4)
- Elisha's raising the life of the Shunammite's son (2 Kg 4)
- Elisha purifies the deadly stew (2 Kg 4)

- Elisha heals Naaman of leprosy (2 Kg 5)
- Gehazi gets leprosy for his deception (2 Kg 5)
- Elisha recovers the axe head (2 Kg 6)
- Elisha shows the horses and chariots of fire (2 Kg 6)
- The miraculous defeat of the Syrians (2 Kg 7)
- The defeat of the Assyrians by the Angel of the Lord (2 Kg 19)
- The reversal of the sun as a sign to Hezekiah (2 Kg 20)

The Books of First and Second Chronicles details some of the miracles written in the books of Kings but add others, such as fire from heaven at the dedication of the Temple. There are many prophetic words and times when the hand of God was obviously upon his people for their good, but the most notable miracles among the prophets were those in the Book of Daniel.

- Daniel's many dream interpretations (Dan)
- Daniel's knowledge of Nebuchadnezzar's dream and the interpretation (Dan 2)
- Shadrach, Meshach, and Abednego's survival of the fiery furnace (Dan 3)
- Nebuchadnezzar's humiliation and restoration (Dan 4)
- The handwriting on the wall (Dan 5)

- Daniel's survival in the lions' den (Dan 6)

This has been a brief account of God's miraculous intervention in the Old Testament. The striking thing is not how often miracles were done, but how seldom. God is usually content to work through and upon mankind by the natural course, at least in that particular dispensation. It should encourage us that God could seem to be silent for long periods, only to enter in at just the right moment for the sake of his people. We will see as we look at the New Testament and Church history that God continues to this.

CHAPTER 4

MIRACLES IN THE LIFE OF JESUS

What follows will be a brief chronicle of *some* of the miracles performed by Jesus and his Church in the Scriptural accounts. Once again, the scope of this book allows for only an introductory treatment of these events.

The Greatest Miracle

J.I. Packer, in his great book *Knowing God,* says, "It is here, in the thing that happened at the first Christmas, that the most profound unfathomable depths of the Christian revelation lie. God became man. Nothing in fiction is as fantastic as this truth of the incarnation" (53). Packer rightly points out that no miracle performed by Jesus should be difficult to believe if one can only come to terms with the fact that God in heaven became flesh, was born of a virgin and dwelt among us. So that is where we start, with an angel and a virgin (Lk 1:26-38 ESV).

God had been silent about this story for nearly five hundred years. Just like the Jews were bound in slavery for 430 years in Egypt, waiting for salvation, they were bound in dispersion and eventually oppressed by Rome for even longer, again, as they waited for salvation. Then God began to speak again. First, he sent his angel, a messenger of God, to the parents of John the Baptist to foretell that Elizabeth, a cousin of Mary, who was barren and old, would bear a son. This child is the one who Isaiah said would be the "voice crying out in the wilderness to prepare the way of the Lord" (Isa 40:3). When Zechariah, her husband, showed a measure of disbelief, the angel struck him with dumbness for the gestation period. He opened his mouth again at the birth and the naming of his son.

God was moving. He was up to something great, and he was showing that signs and wonders would accompany this new age. The angel then appeared to the young virgin, betrothed to Joseph, to announce to her that she would bear a Son from the Holy Spirit. It was one thing for Zechariah and Elizabeth to have a child, but this virgin birth was another altogether new!

Even more miraculous than the conception of Christ to a virgin was the very fact that God the Son would appear.

And the Word became flesh and dwelt among us, and we have seen his glory, glory as of the only Son from the Father, full of grace and truth (Jn 1:14, ESV).

The Word of God, the Logos, the very power of God in the form of his Son, would leave his heavenly throne and become a baby to a humble family. The wonder of wonders! Then he was born in Bethlehem; the shepherds in a nearby field were told the good news and given the sign of a mighty angel chorus in the sky. The magi brought gifts because they followed the star in the east and were given dreams about where to go and to avoid Herod, who will kill the baby.

The Helping Miracles

God did not record the miracles that surrounded the boy Jesus as he grew up in the Holy canon. But as soon as we see Jesus as an adult, it is clear that signs and wonders would be a fixture of his ministry. All the miracles of Jesus are signs of the already-and-not-yet kingdom of God. At Jesus' baptism, a voice from heaven speaks and says, "This is my beloved Son, with whom I am well pleased" (Mt 3:17, ESV). This itself is a miracle, but God and his Son were just getting started! The Holy Spirit then led Jesus into the wilderness to do what Adam had been unable to do, defeat Satan and his temptations. Then he began to preach. Luke tells us that Jesus kicked off his program with a dramatic scene in the synagogue. Having taken the scroll of Isaiah, he read:

"The Spirit of the Lord is upon me, because he has anointed me to proclaim good news to the poor. He has sent me to proclaim liberty to the captives and recovering of sight to the blind, to set at liberty those who are oppressed, to proclaim the year of the Lord's favour." And he rolled up the scroll and gave it back to the attendant and sat down. And the eyes of all in the synagogue were fixed on him. And he began to say to them, "Today this Scripture has been fulfilled in your hearing" (Luke 4:18-21, ESV).

And this is the clue to the reason for the miracles of Jesus. He will "proclaim liberty to the captives" (the sign of deliverance), "recovering of sight to the blind" (the sign of healing), "to set at liberty those who are oppressed" (the signs of deliverance and salvation), and "to proclaim the year of the Lord's favour" (the signs of salvation and feeding of the masses). And rightfully proclaimed, "this Scripture [is] fulfilled."

Most of the miracles that Jesus performed were helping miracles. Jesus did not bend the laws of nature to be glorified and bring glory to God only; his desire was to help. This was a sign in itself of God's compassion for those that are hurt, marginalized, and broken. Jesus went about doing that.

John tells us that his first miracle was at a wedding in Cana (Jn 2). The hosts had run out of wine and faced a major social problem. Jesus' mother was sensitive to their plight and asked her Son to intervene, though it seems he had no intention of doing anything at that point. Nevertheless, he did what she asked and saved the newlyweds from shame. This was a helping sign, but it had the effect of impressing his disciples, and John records that, "This, the first of his signs, Jesus did at Cana in Galilee, and manifested his glory. And his disciples believed in him" (Jn 2:11, ESV).

Why did Jesus perform so many signs and wonders? It authenticated his proclamation of the kingdom of God in a generation that needed it. Jesus was radical and had a very different ministry from the religious teachers of the day. So it makes sense that God would authenticate his message for the sake of those who would believe, to help them do so, and, sadly, for the sake of those who would not, so there could be no doubt that their rejection of Christ was wilful stubbornness to believe what God was making plain. Those who hear of Jesus and reject him are held accountable but imagine how much worse it is for those who see him with their own eyes and yet do not believe.

The helping miracles are apparent. Jesus spent his days healing the sick, casting out demons, feeding the masses, and raising the dead. He seemed to help almost arbitrarily. This should be a lesson for his Church. We should not discriminate too much in who we help with our resources and our prayers. God will sort out who comes into his kingdom, but we must *show* it to everyone, not only by signs and wonders but by the more *natural* methods as well so that we can authenticate that which we proclaim: the kingdom of God and it's crucified and risen, King!

The Miracles of Proof

Aside from the myriad of helping miracles, there were the wonders that were mostly designed to show his glory and authenticate his claim that he is God the Son.

These include his control of the weather, his ability to walk on top of the water, and even his extreme prophetic knowledge at times. These miracles had an effect like the one expressed after Jesus calmed the storm: "And the men marveled, saying, "What sort of man is this, that even winds and the sea obey him" (Mt 8:27, ESV).

The Miracle of the Resurrection

Of course, the greatest miracle of Jesus was the death that destroyed death, and the resurrection, which, like all of Jesus' miracles, was a miracle performed by the Holy Spirit. The miracle of Jesus' death was that he was able to take our sin into his flesh and bear the wrath of God for it. The miracle of the resurrection was to authenticate the power of his death. Those who turn to Christ today for salvation still do so because they believe in this miracle. Without a belief in this one, in particular, there can be no salvation. This miracle, like all the others, was and is for the sake of drawing all men and women who would believe and leave it to God for his great salvation.

CHAPTER 5

MIRACLES IN THE HISTORY OF THE CHURCH, STARTING WITH THE APOSTLES

Many would be willing to believe that Jesus Christ, the Son of God, was a miracle worker. That it is only Jesus and no one else who performed miracles. For the rest of us, we must focus on the *natural* blessings of God. That is a convenient position to take, which requires very little faith. But that is not the reality. The reality is that the church has always had the same power to do signs and wonders as her groom, Jesus, does, and for the same purposes of helping people, and more importantly, showing the reality of the favour of God in Christ. This begins in the Gospels with the commissioning and empowering of the twelve chosen disciples of Jesus.

These twelve were sent out by Jesus. He instructed them, *"Go nowhere among the Gentiles and enter no town of the Samaritans but go rather to the lost sheep of the house of Israel. And proclaim as you go, saying, 'The kingdom of heaven is at hand.' Heal the sick, raise the dead, cleanse lepers, cast out demons. You received without paying; give without pay" (Mt 10:5-8, ESV).*

Jesus had a specific mission for the disciples to go before him into various places and do what he had been doing: showing and proclaiming the kingdom of God. How? By helping people through miracles. "Heal the sick, raise the dead, cleanse lepers, cast out demons." It shows us that Jesus not only came to do these things, but he also empowered his people to do them as well. The reason for all this is given by a clue in the last verse of that same section:

Truly, I say to you, it will be more bearable on the Day of Judgment for the land of Sodom and Gomorrah than for that town (Mt 10:15, ESV).

This was said of those towns that saw the signs, heard the message, and rejected Jesus by rejecting his messengers. The power of God was to leave little doubt of the truth. The signs were a blessing to those who accepted them, a curse and judgment for those who, knowing the truth, would reject it.

Before one could protest that this was only for the special twelve, remember that Jesus expanded the Church's reach when he gave the same commission and the same empowerment to the seventy-two.

After this, the Lord appointed seventy-two others and sent them on ahead of him, two by two, into every town and place where he was about to go...*Whenever you enter a town, and they receive you, eat what is set before you. Heal the sick in it and say to them, "The kingdom of God has come near to you" (Lk 10:1, 8-9, ESV).*

Again, the reason becomes clear at the end when Jesus pronounces judgment on the towns that reject his message.

Pentecost

After the resurrection and ascension of Jesus (yet another sign), the Apostles obey the order to wait in Jerusalem for the Holy Spirit to come from heaven. Then in Acts 2, we see another miracle.

When the day of Pentecost arrived, they were all together in one place. And suddenly there came from heaven a sound like a mighty rushing wind, and it filled the entire house where they were sitting. And divided tongues as of fire appeared to them and rested on each one of them. And they were all filled with the Holy Spirit and began to speak in other tongues as the Spirit gave them utterance (Act 2:1-4, ESV).

And then people from many different nations heard the mighty works of God proclaimed in their own tongues,

And all were amazed and perplexed, saying to one another, "What does this mean?" But others mocking said, "They are filled with new wine" (Acts 2:12-13, ESV).

After this day, not only were the disciples' new men, but they were filled with the power of God. This power was given for the same kind of ministry that they had seen their Lord fulfill. Theirs would be the show-and-tell ministry of the kingdom of God. They would show that the kingdom of God had come, and then they would proclaim it, explaining what people were seeing them do. This was in fulfillment of the promise of Christ:

"Truly, truly, I say to you, whoever believes in me will also do the works that I do; and greater works than these will he do because I am going to the Father" (Jn 14:12, ESV).

Peter preaches immediately after the outpouring of the Holy Spirit, and three thousand are saved. When one sinner repents and is granted new life, it is a miracle. This was the miracle of regeneration on a large scale. Afterward, signs and wonders were a regular occurrence.

Observe: And they devoted themselves to the apostles' teaching and the fellowship, to the breaking of bread and the prayers. And awe came upon every soul, and many wonders and signs were being done through the apostles. And all who believed were together and had all things in common (Acts 2:42-44, ESV).

Peter and John heal a lame beggar after that and are arrested. Not all the miracles were happy ones. In Acts 5, we witness the tragic story of Ananias and Sapphira, who lied to the Apostles about their giving, and for no great reason. They both dropped dead, and fear of God came on the Church.

Acts 5:12 says that many signs and wonders were being done all the time. Then after a disciple named Stephen is arrested and killed, another deacon in the church, Phillip, is commanded by the voice of God to go and preach to a eunuch from Ethiopia, before being teleported away!

Saul, later Paul, was converted next by a visit from Jesus, which first left him blind, but then he was healed by another disciple. Peter healed a paralyzed man, Aeneas, and many were converted as a result. Immediately after that, Peter brought Dorcas back to life, and so, *"Many believed in the Lord" (Acts 9:42, ESV).*

Space doesn't permit me to go on, but Paul's ministry was characterized by the same power. This was the way God chose to start his church. He deemed it necessary, just as today it is sometimes considered necessary for him to show his glory and the truth of the Gospel through signs and wonders.

After Acts

Though our sources for miracles after the completion of the canon are not the inspired and holy Word of God, they can be trusted in the same way historians trust historical documents and accounts. Through historical documents, one can know how England was built, Historians have their methods of authenticating information. What follows are some very brief accounts of the miraculous intervention of God in the history of the growth of Jesus' church. I will include here what church historians have seen as reasonably valid.

From various documents, it is clear that those who have studied the phenomenon of the rise of Christianity attributed it to the signs and wonders that would accompany the preaching of the gospel. In 235 AD, Hippolytus of Rome wrote:

"These gifts were first bestowed upon us, the apostles, when we were about to preach the gospel to every creature [...] for the conviction of unbelievers, that those who the word did not persuade, the power of signs might put to shame; for signs are not for us who believe, but for the unbelievers, both for the Jews and Gentiles" [Michael Green, Evangelism in the Early Church (Grand Rapids, MI: Eerdmans, 1970), 192.].

The great church father Augustine of Hippo said, "I should not be a Christian, but for the miracles" (Blaise Pascal, Pensées, sec. 13, "The Miracles.").

Iraneus, who was a student of Polycarp, who was a student of John the Apostle, attributed the great success in preaching and expanding the Church to the miracle of deliverance from unclean spirits. In his famous book, *The Decline and Fall of the Roman Empire*, Edward Gibbon said this: [T]he supernatural gifts very frequently brought about the conviction of infidels [...] unbelievers" [Edward Gibbon, The Decline and Fall of the Roman Empire, Vol . 1 (New York, NY: Harper & Brothers Publishers, 1879), 505–6, 539–40].

It is clear that God continued his program of authenticating the message of the church, although they were hated by the world in the early days.

After the Roman Empire embraced the faith in the fourth century, there is markedly less miraculous activity. Is this because God did not think it was necessary? Is it because the power of the church was diluted by forced conversions; that is, was the church full of unbelievers? When being a Christian meant likely martyrdom, it seemed miracles accompanied them. When it did not, it seems the power of God for wonders was proportionally diminished, whether by God, lack of true faith, or both.

The Middle Ages and the Reformation

Just like in the Old Testament history of the people of God, the history of the church comes with long seasons of dryness in terms of signs and wonders. This is what I mean, there are many reported miracles throughout the history of the church over 2000 years, but in the Middle Ages, one tragic turn was that the church became superstitious. Rather than glorify God properly for any miracle, they became obsessed with bones and artifacts of the saints who supposedly performed some miracle. This, as one could imagine, came with fraud, since it was extremely profitable to be the owner of one of these relics.

After the Protestant Reformation in the 16th century, writers began to condemn the use of miracles in the medieval church, claiming that the age of miracles had long ceased and that whatever the church claimed as signs and wonders must have been the works of Satan or just hoaxes. Men like John Calvin argued that they were necessary for the brand new church, but now that the Bible was complete, God expected his people to turn the Word of God in faith, without the need for "proof."

The Catholics, in turn, claimed that the Reformers were only trying to justify the fact that God was *not* authenticating their own message. Which was true. Indeed, the Reformation did not seem to be born and driven by signs. It was more driven by doctrine and backlash against the abuses of the church prior.

Was the church now guilty of preaching her experience, and *not* the Word of God? Or was it really true that God simply chose not to move in that sort of way for that season? The church was blessed at that time and strengthened. Over the next three hundred years, there were several revivals and awakenings, but the main miracle was that of regeneration. It is hard to find credible evidence of healing, deliverance, or other signs and wonders in the history of the western church at this time.

One notable exception was the Methodism of John Wesley. It was reported that "many individuals in London, Oxford and Bristol reported supernatural healings, visions, dreams, spiritual impressions, power in evangelizing, [and] extraordinary bestowments of wisdom" [Živadinović, Dojcin (2015). "Wesley and Charisma: An Analysis of John Wesley's View of Spiritual Gifts". Andrews University Seminary Student Journal. 1 (2): 53–71.]. Wesley himself believed in a doctrine of *continuationism,* stating that spiritual gifts are meant for today and accompany great holiness and piety.

The Twentieth Century Charismatic Movement

If it is true that God moves by his Spirit in waves throughout church history and today, then the beginning of the twentieth century brought a new wave of his power. A notable starting point is Azusa, California, in 1906 with a three-year revival. Nightly, it was reported that dramatic healings, tongues-speaking, and mass salvations occurred. There were lighting boltlike surges of the Holy Spirit's power, which knocked participants to the ground. There is one fantastic story of fire hovering over the building. The fire department showed up, only to find the building unconsumed.

Whatever one thinks of the authenticity of these accounts, they are widespread, and several modern Pentecostal movements were born there, which eventually found their way into the mainstream denominations. Catholicism, Anglicanism, and Evangelicalism all shot forth branches of charismatic waves. All this came with some good and bad stuff. There has been much criticism of some of the manifestations, and scholars still debate the source: God or Satan, the Holy Spirit, or man's mind? But there can be little doubt for anyone who looks seriously into it that God was moving in some way in signs and wonders again. There are stories today in 2020 of healing, raising the dead, and various manifestations of God's power. In the next chapter, I will detail a select few experiences narrated to me by pastors and believers.

CHAPTER 6

MIRACLES TODAY

We have looked at the role that miracles played in the Old Testament, beginning with the miracle of the creation of the world out of nothing. We followed the story of the Jews and lightly touched on most of the well-known miracles in their redemptive history. We saw the miraculous life and ministry of Jesus and noted how he expected his disciples to minister in the same way. Lastly, we looked at the history of the church from Acts 2 to recent times. We have seen that, just like in the days of the Bible, God chose certain seasons for his miraculous intervention, and that signs and wonders have never wholly ceased from being part of the Christian experience, particularly when evangelism is a priority.

In this chapter, I'd like to detail a few miracles either in my own experience or those I have heard from people I know personally, especially Pastor Matt from the USA. In my previous book on healing, I wrote several healing miracles that you can refer to. In this book, we shall not only look at a few healing miracles, but we shall also look at miracles of provision.

A church in the U.S. held its church meeting in a school. Everything was looking up, and they were beginning to reach many people for Christ. The pastor ensured to pay rent before each semester. One day the pastor went to pay rent, but when he got there, the administrator sheepishly told him that he had rented it out to another church. Since the other church was willing to pay more, the administrator had given them the space, but had not notified the pastor about the changes.

The pastor had only thirty days to vacate the premises. It had been a difficult task to find this meeting space in the first place. The team tasked with finding a location had looked for something within their meager budget all over town with no luck. The pastor had to stop everything so that he could focus on finding a building. Full of anxiety, he drove to a nearby park and sat down on a bench to pray. As he prayed, God spoke to him. The voice was not audible, but it was unmistakable and came with a powerful sense of peace and warmth.

"Don't wear yourself out looking for a building. In fact, don't look for a building. Fast and pray. Ask the church to fast and pray. I will provide it. Don't stop doing my work to find a rental space."

With this voice came an infusion of faith that impressed the pastor. He immediately called the leadership team and relayed the message. The team was full of confidence and began to fast at lunchtime every day to pray for a worship space.

The pastor had to remind himself *not* to go looking for a building so many times. Anytime he became anxious, he prayed, and God supplied the strength for the next day. One particular Sunday, when the church was gathered in the old space for the last time, the pastor told the whole church to pray for the building. He told them how God had impressed him to keep doing ministry, and he would provide the space.

After the service, a man walked up to him and said, *"I know why I'm here now. I work at another church, but when I woke up this morning, I felt led to come here. Our church was preparing to rent the old downtown movie theatre that was previously rehabbed and reopened, but we decided not to. You should call them tomorrow. They will be eager to have you rent it for your service."*

The movie theatre was a beautiful space and a perfect place to relocate to. Interestingly the pastor had tried to rent the space, but the owner had adamantly refused.

"No, way! We're not renting this space to a church" was the answer the Pastor got when he approached the owner the first time.

Had something changed? It turned out that times were hard for the theatre, and they weren't generating enough revenue. They were desperate. When the pastor called the next day, the owner eagerly rented the building to him for one-third of the price they had been paying for the school! Within a year after the church began using the space, the theatre went out of business. It ended up in the hands of the bank, who continued to rent it to the church for the same price, only now, the church could have access to it seven days a week, rather than moving in and out on Sundays! God had indeed provided.

Later, it was learned that the vice president of the bank in charge of the building had plans to kick the church out, but whenever he would try to do it, he just couldn't make himself do it. It appeared that God was prevailing over him, though he was not a Christian. With time, the church grew and saw dozens of people give their lives to Christ in that place. They went from one service each Sunday to two before moving to a larger space.

Another church was going through financial trouble and was considering what changes to make to pay the bills. Staff members would likely be laid off. Important programs would be cut. As they were having a prayer meeting one day, God revealed to them that he did not want cuts to be made, but that they should have a special offering in the church. 250 people regularly attended the church. As they prayed, a vision took shape. The whole church was to raise $250,000 to reach its target. Could the church raise so much? An announcement was made, and the church was asked to pray for the $250,000. And for God to reveal to each of them how much they should give.

When the day arrived for the offering, the church was faithful, and they gave sacrificially. But when the money was counted, it was only $220,000, which was surely a blessing and would keep the church running at full speed. But as they puzzled over how they missed the number, someone pointed out that they should look again at the number of people attending. There were two Sunday morning services at the church, and many people had to attend both because of their areas of service. An equation was used to account for that fact so that they weren't counted twice. When this was investigated, it turned out the equation was misapplied. How many people do you think were *actually attending* service each week? You probably guessed right.....two hundred twenty! They did not know that they were wrong about the numbers, and we're actually spending more than they should because of miscalculation. But God knew the exact number of people that were coming and adjusted accordingly!

Prophecy

One form of miracle that is common in Jesus' church is the miracle of a prophetic word. A pastor had a member of his church who was committed to keeping the Torah and Jewish laws. Christians believe that Jesus came as the fulfillment of the ceremonial law, and that is why we no longer eat a certain way to please God, or wear tassels on our clothes, keep Jewish festivals and holidays.

But some teach that besides the Gospel, a person needs works of the law to make God happy. This heresy has been in place since the Book of Acts. The pastor and this member had debated about this for months, but the pastor could not get through to the man.

One day when the pastor was leading a prayer night that this particular member was attending with his wife and children, the pastor asked if he could lay hands on the man and pray for him. This was a common occurrence in this church, so the man was eager to allow it. The pastor was praying various things over the man, and it appeared that the Holy Spirit was moving on the man.

He was trembling slightly under the move of the Holy Spirit's power.

At one point, the words popped into the mind of the pastor, "Romans 2:12." The pastor did not know what verse that was. He was unsure if it was really God, but he took a risk and spoke it out, saying, "I'm hearing the verse Romans 2:12." Maybe it is just my imagination, but let's look it up and see if it means anything to you.

Both men were dumbfounded when they read, *"For all who have sinned without the law will also perish without the law, and all who have sinned under the law will be judged by the law."* The pastor was actually embarrassed because he didn't want the man to think that he had "staged" it. But he was also amazed. If the pastor was amazed, the man was even more surprised and rightly terrified. He renounced his extra-religious ways that very night and was likely saved. God had so loved this man and his family that he gave that miraculous word as a warning straight from him!

Healing

In my previous book, *Empowering Healing and Hope Through Faith*, I wrote about the manifestation of the Kingdom of God through healing miracles, both in the life of Jesus and the Apostles and in the lives of believers today. Here are two more stories of healing miracles.

My friend recently shared with me that last year his seventy-year-old father had a high fever that would not come down. Eventually, his blood count began to drop rapidly, so they rushed him to the hospital for treatment. The doctors diagnosed him with a viral fever that they called dengue.

After three days, the fever went away, and they were hopeful that he had recovered. But on the fourth day, he once again fell ill. This time around, they realized that he not only had dengue, but he was also jaundiced. His fever was so intense that he began to suffer brain damage, losing all his memory and eventually his consciousness. The situation continued to worsen.

After an MRI, the doctors pronounced his brain permanently damaged and said that it would be difficult for him to recover. The fever had caused severe injuries. The man's family had only one recourse at this point, to trust God and pray for a miracle. According to my friend, they constantly prayed, proclaiming with faith the words, "Nothing is impossible for you, Lord." Unable to walk, the doctors prescribed a wheelchair for the man.

My friend admits that at one point, they began to lose all hope, but they never gave up on their prayers. His father started shouting abuses at the hospital staff and seemed to be getting worse. The family was in emotional agony, watching their beloved father deteriorate. They continued to pray, and God eventually led them to another doctor who continued to treat him. Everything changed at this point. All the effects of the illness, previously thought to be unrepairable, were reversed.

The doctors said he would not get his memory back, but God restored his memory. They said he would not walk, but he is walking ten laps a day at the nearby track. God is the great physician. We may lose hope, but God never does. My friend is ecstatic to report that this situation has given him a rock-solid faith in Jesus Christ, the great healer.

Another friend, a young lady, told me a fantastic story. I'm going to include it here in her words:

"Praise the Lord. Though I was born and brought up in a Christian family, I was neither obedient, nor was I disciplined in spiritual matters. One day, everything changed. On 24th December 2016, my mother told me not to go outside, but I didn't listen. I went out for a bike ride on a highway without wearing a helmet with my younger brother. I don't remember what hit us, but my brother and I found ourselves lying in the middle of the road. I clearly remember that I had passed away due to the injury on my head, but a bright flash of light came in front of me, and I felt like someone pulled me back to life by offering their hand. That someone is my Creator, Jesus Christ. I woke up all over a sudden and saw many people gathered around, but no one helped us.

We rode to the nearby hospital on the same broken bike. With minor injuries on our bodies, everyone in the hospital told us it was a miracle that we both had survived the crash. It is because of God's mercy, help, and favour that we were alive that day. We were told to take x-rays and scans, but to our surprise, my brother was told that he had no significant injury, and I was told I had minor fractures. The Lord has been so merciful and gracious to me, that even those small fractures were cured within 3 weeks, and I was back to normal.

A year later, I met someone who came up and prophesied to me saying, the devil wanted to destroy and kill me last year through an accident, but Jesus gave me life because the things that the Lord has in store for me are much greater than I could ever imagine. That one night, a day before Christmas back in the year 2016 changed my life completely. I live a healthy life today by the mercy of God. I could have died, but my creator gave me life. I realized then that without Jesus, I'm nothing! I had a fresh start. If God can choose a person like me, who was always disobedient, if he can bring me back to life, then He can do wonders in your life too. Praise God!"

As you can see, the result of these healing miracles is a renewed faith and glory to God. In the first story, the one who witnessed his father healed has had a revitalized faith. In the second, the one who was healed will never be the same again, going from weak and disobedient in faith, to strong, purposeful, and committed to God.

Revelation Produces Faith

It is my prayer that the testimonies I have shared in this chapter will open your spiritual eyes and understanding so that you can see that God wants you well. These people's lives will never be the same again because they have received a profound revelation of God's power. There is hope for you too. You don't have to keep on suffering from that debilitating disease when Jesus has already healed you.

Jesus said we shall know the truth, and it will set us free *(John 8:32)*. It is by knowing the truth that we are set free from all the traps and bondages that the enemy is trying to set us in. Religion has made people accept and tolerate things that Jesus already paid for at the cross. But as we have seen through these testimonies that miracles happen today just the way they did in the past.

You don't have to accept and settle for less than what your heavenly Father wants you to have. He has so much in store for you if you will only trust and surrender yourself to him. Even though the enemy intended to harm you, let God use whatever challenge you are facing today to display His splendor and love to and through you.

Yes, it may be difficult for you right now, but if you commit to what God is trying to reveal to you through these testimonies, your faith will be stirred up, and you will start to see miracles powerfully manifesting in your life. You don't have to settle for less because Jesus came so that you can have life more abundantly.

The enemy would like to isolate and make you believe that you are the only one that is struggling with that disease or issue. If that is what he has been doing to you, then you can see that he is a liar. So many people have gone through different challenges, but as you can see from these stories that they overcame, and you can too.

God's Love: the Key to Living a Miraculous Life

There is one key point that I would love you to take and run with it from this book until you see miracles happening in your life, and that is *God loves you unconditionally*. There is nothing you have done, or you will ever do that will cause you to earn the love of your heavenly Father. See, God doesn't love us when we are good and hate us when we are wrong. He loves us with all our flaws.

Okay, why is it essential for you to know about God's love, given that you just want to experience miracles in your life? Well, knowing that the creator of heaven and earth loves you unconditionally will help you understand why you qualify for healing miracles today.

It will help you know his heart for all his children and why he wants you to live in divine health and prosperity. When you understand why and how much God loves you, it will be easy for you to expect your healing miracle today. It will be easy for you to understand the next chapters in this book.

He who Did Not Spare His Own Son

I would like you to take a minute and think about all the things that are happening in the world today. Think about how people are living their lives. Turn on the television, and you will see how much blasphemy is in the world. Look at how people are abusing the temple of God and calling it fun. Now, would you give up your only son to die on the cross for these people? Can you allow your only child to pay for the sins of the world even though you know that some of them will never acknowledge you or what you have done for them?

When Jesus was on the cross, he cried out to his Father and asked him why he had forsaken him. But God turned away from his son so that you and I could be saved and enjoy eternal life. Not just that, he did it so that we could live in good health, freedom, and walk in every spiritual blessing that we have been given in heavenly places. Pause and think about that for a second.

What great love! The best part, he did that without expecting anything in return. See, God can do great all by himself, but because he is love and we are the objects of his love, he was willing to stoop to our levels so that we can be set free from sin. Jesus, the son of God, left the comfort of heaven to come and save us from eternal damnation. He came to his own people, but they rejected him. We have also rejected him from time to time. Some of us are rejecting him right now by rejecting his great sacrifice on the cross. Sad, right?

Focus on God's Love and Live Miraculously

Many Christians know that healing is part of the atonement. Many of us know that God has blessed us in every way. But let's be honest, only a few Christians can attest to living miraculous lives. Why is that? It is because the enemy has convinced us to look at our shortcomings instead of God's love. We have been told that we need to earn God's blessings and love. But the key to living a miraculous life is God's love. The key to loving and trusting God is found in his love for us. When you're rooted and grounded in his love, it will be difficult for the enemy to steal your healing miracle and destroy your faith.

You were created out of love. Now, it may not look like it in the natural realm, but when God formed in your mother's womb, he did it out of love. Not just that, but he had good plans for you even before you were knit in that womb. God's plans are meant to prosper you and not to fail you. Sickness is not a plan from God because it is not meant to prosper you but to fail you. Don't embrace it, instead of fight against it through faith.

CHAPTER 7

EXPECT YOUR HEALING MIRACLE TODAY: WHAT GOD PROMISES HE DELIVERS

But he was wounded for our transgressions, he was bruised for our iniquities: the chastisement of our peace was upon him; and with his stripes we are healed. Isaiah 53:5(KJV)

You are in so much pain. The sickness in your body is slowing you down. You can barely do the things that you love. Maybe you are on the verge of losing your job, or your loved ones have abandoned you because of the condition that you are in.

It could be that you have used up all your finances on medication. It has been a journey from one doctor to another, and you are on the verge of giving up. You do not want to live like this anymore.

Well, you are not alone. All of us struggle with health issues at some point. But you don't have to feel that way anymore, child of God. Expect your healing miracle today and start living an abundant life, *for what God promises he delivers.*

Why do we Struggle with Sickness and Disease?

Fallen World

We live in a fallen world, and that means that we will face challenges from time to time. These challenges come in the form of financial, physical, mental, and emotional issues. So sickness is part of the fallen world.

Not Taking Good Care of Our Bodies

Much as we live in a fallen world, sometimes we fall sick because we do not take good care of our bodies. See yourself as a steward of the things that God has given you, and that includes your body. You need to take good care of yourself so that God can use you to fulfil the plans he has for you.

Your body is the temple of God, and the Holy Spirit dwells in it ***(1 Corinthians 6:19-20)***. So be careful of how you take care of it. Eat healthy meals and always take some time off to rest.

Spiritual Attack

Sometimes we struggle with sickness and disease because we are under spiritual attack. As believers, we know that we are in a battle, and the enemy does not want us to fulfill the purposes of God in this world. So there are times he's going to attack your body to slow you down or stop you from accomplishing the purposes of God in this world.

Why you should expect a Healing Miracle Today

Jesus has paid for your Divine Health

Your heavenly Father did not spare his own son ***(Romans 8:32)***. So why should he refuse to heal you when Jesus paid for your health at the scourging post? Please stop feeling sorry for yourself and expect your miracle today because it is legally yours. There are so many healing promises in the Bible that you can stand on. God will never promise you something and then refuse to give it to you. He is a faithful Father. He watches over his word.

The Devil is Defeated

The enemy was defeated at the cross 2000 years ago. He does not have any legal rights over your life. Since you gave your life to Christ, God removed you from the kingdom of darkness and transferred you to the kingdom of his son. You do not belong to the devil, you're not under his control.

What does this mean?

It means that you are healed. When the enemy attacks your body with sickness and disease, he's doing that to steal the divine health that you have been given by Jesus. Remember, he is a thief. You should not accept that, you need to fight from the point of victory because the war has already been won at the cross. ***(John 10:10)***

There are stories of God healing people from sickness and disease in the Old Testament and the New Testament. It means that healing miracles are God's will for our lives.

Healing Miracles in the Bible

The Woman with the Issue of Blood

She had gone from one physician to another. But all the treatments that she got did not stop her from bleeding. If anything, she lost her finances. But then she heard about Jesus, a man who would heal every manner of sickness and disease. He was her last hope, and she was willing to risk her life just so she could get her healing.

When she touched the hem of the garment of Jesus, she stopped bleeding immediately. ***Like this woman, you can receive your healing miracle today if you only turn to Jesus and believe that he is able and willing to heal you***. Maybe you've used up all your savings. Perhaps you've tried it all, and Jesus is your last hope. Turn to Jesus just like this woman did and know that he will not disappoint you. ***(Luke 8:43-48)***

The Leper

A man covered with leprosy approached Jesus and asked him to heal him if he was willing. Jesus reached out to him, told the man he was willing, and healed him. Now, in those times, lepers were seen as outcasts. So, while the man knew that Jesus was able to heal, he wasn't sure that he would be willing to heal a leper.

Maybe you think that God will not heal you because of a sin you committed. It could be that you are looked at as an outcast by your loved ones because of the kind of disease that you have. Here is the thing, there is now no more condemnation for you're in Christ Jesus.

Remember, nothing is too big or small for God. The way Jesus was willing to heal the leper is the same way he's willing to heal you today. You only need to turn to him and ask him to heal you. ***(Luke 5:12-14)***

The Blind man at Bethsaida

People brought a blind man to Jesus at Bethsaida and begged him to heal him. He took the man out of the village, spit on his eyes, and asked him if he saw. The man told Jesus that he saw men as trees, so Jesus put his hands on the man again, and his sight was restored.

It could be that you have prayed for a very long time to receive healing in your body, but nothing has worked out. You feel so discouraged because it did not work out the first time. Yes, you want to claim your healing, but you don't think it will work out as it did not work out last time.

Or maybe you have been standing firm on the healing promises. You have been expecting it to manifest for a very long time, but that hasn't happened yet. You're beginning to doubt whether healing is for today.

Do not be discouraged. You may not have received your healing miracle instantly like the blind man at Bethsaida, but know that your healing will come today. You only need to stand firm in faith and believe. ***(Mark 8:22-25)***

How to Receive Your Healing Miracle Today

Stand firm in the word of God

I know the pain in your body seems so real right now. But you need to know that the word of God is true. The Bible says you were healed, it means that the pain in your body is a lie from the pit of hell. You need to stand firm in the word of God.

Resolve in your heart that you are going to stand firm in the word of God until healing manifests in your body. See, you are not a sick person trying to get healed, you are a healed person that is fighting for the health that the enemy is trying to steal. Now how do you react when someone tries to take what rightfully belongs to you?

You fight back, right?

But here is the thing; you cannot fight back without the word of God. It is only by knowing the word of God that we are able to know the will of God over our lives and stand firm in the faith that God has given us. Look for Bible verses about healing, study, and meditate on them until they become alive in your heart. Then use them as weapons to fight against the lies of the enemy.

Speak the language of faith

The Bible says that we cannot please God without faith. That means you need faith to receive your healing miracle today. Now here's the thing: you do not need "big faith" to receive a miracle.

Jesus said that if you have faith as small as a mustard seed, then you can tell the mountain to move, and it shall be moved. God has given each of us a measure of faith. That faith will move your mountain that is the sickness or disease in your body. ***(Romans 12:3)***

You need to actively claim your healing

One of the reasons why most Christians struggle to receive healing miracles is that they do not speak the language of faith. If all you do is talk about the pain in your body or how bad the disease is, then you're going to continue in that state of being sick, and the healing miracle will not manifest in your body.

Do not get me wrong. You should not deny the fact that you're in pain. But you should not glorify the pain either. That pain is a fact, but it is not the truth. The truth is Jesus paid for your healing at the scourging post-2000 years ago. Another truth is by his stripes, you are healed. So yes, it's okay to say you're in pain but follow that up by speaking out what Jesus has done for you.

Let your words align with the word of God

A woman had issues with her eyes. Through a friend, she came to learn that Jesus had paid for her healing. She did not have to live like that anymore. The doctor told her that she would eventually lose her sight. The knowledge that Jesus had paid for her healing gave her hope, and she started to stand firm in the word and claim her healing. She ordered her eyes to function according to God's original blueprint, and soon after, she regained her sight. But after some time she started to lose her sight again.

Discouraging right?

Well, not for her! She did not get discouraged; instead, she ordered her eyes to see again, and she regained her sight. Now her vision is perfect.

You need to be intentional about your healing miracle. Do not get discouraged when the devil tries to lie to you. Don't start complaining when that pain comes back into your body; instead, be like the woman in the story, claim your healing. Speak the language of faith, not doubt or fear.

Listen to God

When you look at the Miracles of Jesus, you realize that he did them differently. He healed some people instantly. But there are those he took out of places or told them to go to other places before they received their miracle.

It means that there is no one way for us to receive miracles from God. What may have worked for your friend who had the same disease that you have may not necessarily work for you. You need to be alert in the spirit and listen to what God is telling you to do. Maybe you do not need the whole church to pray for you. You only need to spend time in the word, and healing will manifest in the body. Or maybe you have to call the elders of the church so that they can lay hands on you and anoint you with oil so that you can get healed.

You need to listen to God and follow his voice for your healing miracle to happen today. It could be that you have unforgiveness in your heart that is hindering you from receiving your healing.

All in all, live knowing that healing is for today. Irrespective of what other people believe, you need to let the word of God be your standard. Do not let fear or let the lies of the enemy hinder you from receiving God's best. Stand firm in the word of God, listen to his voice, speak the language of faith, and do not quit until a healing miracle happens in your life today.

Know that God loves you so much, and that is why he gave up his only son to die on the cross for you. He did not do that just so you can have eternal life only but so that you can have abundant life here on earth. Abundant life includes health, so claim your healing today!

Healing Prayer

Father, in the mighty name of Jesus Christ, I want to thank you and worship you today. You are Jehovah Rapha, the Lord, our healer. Thank you for giving up your only son for me so that I can live a healthy life. Lord, I stand firm in your word, which says that you will restore health to me and heal my wounds. I come before your throne boldly to claim my healing in Jesus' name. I command my body to be healed. Pain, leave my body, and be planted in the middle of the sea in Jesus' name. Healing manifest right now in my body!

Almighty God, I also pray for those that are struggling with sickness and disease all over the world. Father, cover them with your wings of healing and help them to enjoy divine health. It is in Jesus' name that I believe and pray, Amen.

CHAPTER 8

WHY ISN'T EVERYONE HEALED?

We have seen the different miracles that have happened from the book of Genesis to the New Testament and also modern-day miracles in previous chapters. We have also learned that God's love is the key to living miraculously and why we should expect healing miracles today. But we may still be struggling to find answers to this one question. *How come some people get healed, and others don't? Why isn't everyone healed?*

It could be that you prayed for someone, but they did not get healed. Or you have struggled with a certain body condition for long. You have prayed, fasted, given, claimed, cast, and bound, but nothing seems to be coming forth. All this has left you confused because you know someone that got healed of the same condition.

In this chapter, we are going to look at some of the things that hinder healing from manifesting in our bodies. We will find out why some people have succumbed to sickness and diseases even though they knew that healing was their portion. So let's begin:

Wrong/False Beliefs

The Bible tells us that Jesus is the same yesterday, today and forever ***Hebrews 13:8***. So how come some people don't get healed today, yet we worship the same Jesus of the Bible? Well, wrong mindsets and beliefs block many of us from receiving healing. Most of us have been told that healing doesn't happen today and so we have grown up believing that we cannot receive healing in our bodies.

Many Christians find it easy to ask God for money, jobs, and other material possessions, but for some reason, they don't believe that God wants them well. It is easier to ask for carnal things than it is for us to believe God for good health because of the wrong mindsets that we have developed over time.

Let's look at some of these wrong beliefs that block us from receiving healing today.

- **God Gives Us Sickness and Disease to Teach Us a Lesson**

Have you ever heard someone say that God gave them some disease to teach them or people around them a lesson? Now, if we are to take time and think about such statements, we will realize that they contradict the word of God. We need to be careful about what we say, hear, and believe. You need to measure what you hear with the word of God. Let the Bible be your standard.

The word of God tells us that every good and perfect gift is from above. Meaning that everything that God gives us is good and perfect. Now take a second and think about this, what is good or perfect about sickness, poverty, or death?

What happens to parents who abuse their children? They are taken to court, and in most cases, they end up losing custody of their children, right? If that is so for us humans, why should we be okay with someone telling us that our heavenly Father gives us a disease to teach us a lesson? In essence, we are agreeing with those people and, most of all, with the enemy that God is a cruel father.

Well, someone may argue that God used to strike people with sickness and disease in the Old Testament. But we need to understand that in those times, people were under the law. If someone broke the law, they would have to suffer the consequences. But thank God for Jesus! Today we are not under the law, but under grace for Jesus has paid for our health, prosperity, freedom, and wholeness at the cross. We have a right standing with God because of Jesus. Healing is part of the atonement.

God is a good father. In fact, the Bible says that God is love, meaning you cannot separate him from love because he is the true definition of love. Now, if God gave up his only son to die for us, why would he give us something that will harm us to teach our loved ones or us a lesson. Most of all, how will you learn the lesson he is trying to teach you when you are dead because of sickness. There are so many ways that our heavenly Father can teach and correct us, but putting sickness and disease in our bodies is not one of those ways.

- **Healing is for Certain People**

Has someone convinced you that healing is for certain people? Are you beginning to buy into the lie that healing is for special people, and you're not one of them? Well, don't allow the enemy to get to you and steal your healing.

Jesus is not a respecter of persons. You are special to God, just like the woman with the issue of blood and that friend or family member who got healed. God wants you well the same way he wants your loved one well because we are all his children. The Bible says he causes the rain to fall on the righteous and the wicked. If God cares for all His creation, why would he refuse to heal you, his beloved child?

A look at *Matthew 12:15* and *Luke 6:19,* and you will see that Jesus healed all who came to him. There is nowhere you see him telling someone to go away because God did not want to heal them. As a matter of fact, the only people that were not healed by are those that did not have faith in him.

If something is not supported by scripture, it is not from God. So there are no special people that have been chosen by God to receive healing. If that was so, it would have been written in the gospels. We are all eligible to receive healing in our bodies because healing is part of the atonement.

- **God hasn't healed you because you lack "big faith"**

"If only my faith was big or strong enough, then God would heal me." Does this statement sound familiar? Or have you heard someone say this? Well, the enemy likes to attack our minds with such lies so that we can feel condemned and stop claiming health and breakthroughs over our bodies. Maybe those are thoughts that keep running in your mind, or you have heard a friend who is sick say this. But this is simply not true. You don't need great faith to receive your healing.

Jesus said if you have faith as small as a mustard seed, then you would say to the mountain to move and it will *(Matthew 17:20)*. Don't wait to have big faith before you can start claiming your healing. God has already given his children a measure of faith, and with that faith, you can say to the sickness in your body to be plucked out by the roots and be gone from your body, and it will move. You can speak to your bank account and command your debts to be supernaturally canceled, and God will open up doors for you to pay off your debt.

Stop looking for great faith and start using the faith that you already have.

Passivity/ Giving Up Quickly

You have prayed and claimed your healing for two weeks or months, but nothing seems to be working. If anything, you're getting worse, and the doctors are telling you to expect the worst. Maybe the person who had the same disease you have just passed away. You are tired of all this, you feel discouraged and just want to quit. It is not God's will for you to be healed, so you think.

Please, before you quit, understand that you are in a battle. Though the enemy has already been defeated at the cross and is going to be judged very soon, he is busy attacking the children of God in the little time that he has left. He is not going to allow you to live in peace. The enemy will not allow you to have that which Jesus died so that you can have easily.

We are told in the Bible that the kingdom of God suffers violence and the violent take it by force *(Matthew 11:12)*. Note that it is the violent, those that are willing to fight and take what God has given to them freely through his son Jesus. You will not win this battle if you let your emotions control you. You need to stand firm in faith and fight! Now, fighting in Christianity means standing firm in the word until you see the manifestation of the promise of God in your life.

You cannot afford to quit right now because it is not God that is withholding miracle healing from you but the enemy. He doesn't want you to enjoy good health. You need to stand firm and fight for that which Jesus died so that you can have.

But it is so hard, you may say.

Let me ask you if you found a snake in your house would you continue living in that house with the snake? No! If you're courageous, you would look for it and kill it, right? If you fear snakes, you will look for someone to come and remove it before setting foot in that house again. But why should you allow sickness to live in your body which is the temple of God? Your body is holy, and the enemy is trying to defile it with sickness. Stop fighting passively and start claiming your healing seriously.

Determine in your heart that you are going to fight this until healing manifests in your body, even if it takes a month or a year. Let the enemy know that you're not backing down without a fight because he is stealing healing from you.

A great example of someone who wasn't passive in the Bible is the woman with the issue of blood. We have already mentioned her in Chapter 7, but let's look at her story again. See, during those times, the law didn't allow people in her condition to interact with others. A woman in her condition was considered unclean. If someone who knew her well saw her in the crowd and revealed her issue to the public before she received healing, she would have been stoned to death.

But this woman was determined to receive her healing. She had probably heard about a man named Jesus from others and had made up her mind to follow and touch the hem of his clothes next time he was in their town. When she heard Jesus was around, she left her house knowing fully well that she was risking her life and started following him. Jesus was her last hope.

Some Bible commentaries say that there were so many people in the place Jesus was that the women crawled to him. Imagine yourself crawling to Jesus to receive healing. To her, it didn't matter as long as she touched the hem of his garment. She had probably heard of people who got healed by simply touching Jesus, and she wanted that for herself.

Today, we don't have to crawl to Jesus to receive healing. We need to stand firm in faith by studying, meditating, and confessing the word of God over our lives until it manifests. You should not give up just because healing doesn't manifest as fast as you thought. Continue standing firm in the promises of God until you see them coming true.

The Kingdom of God is not all about talk but power. God has not given you the spirit of fear but of power. Do not sit on the sidelines passively and expect to experience healing miracles. You need to walk in the power of the Holy Spirit. Pray, stand in faith, fight any lies that the enemy is feeding your mind with the word of God, and don't quit until you see the manifestation of the word of God in your life.

Unbelief

You may be wondering, aren't wrong beliefs the same as unbelief. Well, they are not the same. A person with unbelief believes that it is God's will to heal, but they don't see healing manifesting in their life or their loved ones because they doubt God. On the other hand, a person with wrong beliefs doesn't necessarily believe that it is God's will to heal them.

Understand that having unbelief does not mean that you do not have faith. Most Christians struggle to receive healing because of unbelief. They know that God can heal, but for some reason or another, they struggle to receive that healing in their bodies.

What causes and unbelief?

- **Ignorance**

The Bible says that God's people are destroyed for lack of knowledge. Most times, people will go by what other people have told them about healing. They never take the time to study the word of God and meditate on it. You need to spend time in the word of God so that the Holy Spirit can give you a personal revelation about healing miracles. Maybe you need a miracle right now, and that is where books like this one come in handy. They help you understand God's heart for healing and how to receive healing in your life faster.

But you need to study the word of God because it is a seed. Planting the word of God in your heart through studying and meditation ensures that you receive long term results. Instead of always fighting with sickness and other challenges, the word which is medicine to your body will quicken your body, and you will have sevenfold health.

The word of God is true, and it will never fail you. Spending time studying it will help you understand what God says healing. Don't just quote it because you heard someone else quoting it. The best thing to do is to find where that verse is, study, and meditate until you get revelation from the Holy Spirit about healing. Yes, it sounds like a long process, but it is the best way to deal with ignorance and unbelief.

- **Wisdom of the world**

It is okay to be well-versed with what medical doctors are say about your condition. It comes in handy when you pray because you will know exactly what to rebuke. But the wisdom of the world can also work to your disadvantage as you will be occupied with what the doctors have said more than what God has said in his word.

If all you do is research about the disease you are suffering from to find out what to expect next, then it will be difficult for you to stand in faith. The word of God needs to be more real than what the doctors have said about your condition. Yes, outside circumstances may match what your doctor has said, but you need to read the word of God and allow it to penetrate your heart to the point that you are willing to look foolish in the eyes of people.

Now, having faith doesn't mean that you deny what is going on. Admitting that you have cancer doesn't mean that you have unbelief. But you need to know that the word of God says that by the stripes of Jesus, you were healed, so cancer has nothing on you.

It may be in your body, but it is illegally there. Don't rebuke the doctors for saying you have cancer. But don't allow them to speak death to your body either because Jesus already took that cancer on his body 2000years ago. Let them know that you believe Jesus has healed you.

Instead of feeding yourself with the wisdom of the world, take time to feed the word of God. Avoid watching stuff on TV that will poison your mind and cause you to develop unbelief. Instead, feed yourself with content that will remove unbelief from your heart. Read books about healing, and most of all, turn to the word of God and let God speak to your heart.

In short; the best way to deal with unbelief, wrong beliefs, and passivity is to consider not what the doctors and people around you are saying about your situation. Don't allow other people's words to be more real than what God says in his word. In Romans 4:18 -21, we are told that Abraham did not consider that his own body was dead or that Sarah was barren. Even though Abraham had every reason to doubt the promise of God, he did not consider what he saw with his physical eyes but focused on God's faithfulness.

If Abraham focused on his age and Sarah's barrenness, they would never have gotten Isaac. The enemy will plant negative thoughts in your mind to cause you to doubt. But you don't have to focus on what he's placing in your mind instead focus on what God says. If you have been focusing on what the doctors are saying about your disease, then it is time to shift your focus. Yes, it is hard, but you need to deal with unbelief so that you can enjoy the promises of God in your life.

Overcome unbelief by having a child-like faith. Believe what your heavenly Father says about you is the truth, and consider every other thing a lie.

FINAL THOUGHTS & CONCLUSIONS

It would be unfaithful of us to only believe our experiences and not the word of God. Sadly, this is what happens when the church is not witnessing miracles. John Wimber, a twentieth century pastor in America who was the founder of the Vineyard Movement, tells the story of the beginning of his healing ministry in his book, *Power Healing*.

Having felt that God had called him to preach through the Book of Luke about the kingdom of God, the already/not yet reality of it, he also believed he was to pray for the sick. Every week for ten months he taught the church the Bible on healing and then prayed for the sick. No one was healed. Week after week after week... no one! It was even reported that those who were praying for others were contracting the illnesses of the people they prayed for! One day at the end of the ten months, after nearly half of the church had left over this new obsession with healing that was not happening, Wimber threw himself to the ground and told God he was finished. If God wasn't going to back him up, he wasn't going to tell people that God still heals today.

God spoke to him and said, *"Speak my Word, not your experience."*

That was all. God was telling John that if his Word said that he heals people, then he heals people. So much of the theological error of cessationism is based on the fact that Christians haven't *seen* with their own eyes the kinds of things the Bible describes in the New Testament. So, because of this, they develop a theological perspective that is unbiblical. They say, "I haven't seen miracles, therefore, miracles aren't supposed to happen today." But as God told John Wimber, we are to preach his Word, *not merely* our experiences. If we have not yet experienced what the Bible says is true, that is no excuse to disbelieve it.

John got up and went about his day. The next week, someone called because his wife was terribly ill. John went over there depressed. This guy believed in what John had been teaching, so he had called him. When he went over there he John was praying for her on the outside, but in his mind John was rehearsing his speech on he would have to explain why sometimes God doesn't heal people today. Suddenly, her illness went away. That miracle ignited his faith, John continued to preach and live by the Word of God, and not only his limited experience to that point, God finally began to move.

Why it took ten months, only God knows. Perhaps he was using it to build something important in John. That was the beginning of a powerful ministry of, not only healing, but signs and wonders that accompanied Wimber's preaching for the rest of his days. The lesson here is clear. It is the word of God that is true, *no matter our experience up to this point.* Cultivate a belief in the Bible, and eventually your experience will match.

A Warning

There is a danger here. I have seen Christians and ministries get obsessed with miracles and power, especially if they had seen more of them in the past. But to place the kingdom higher than the King himself, is an error. Will you worship God even if you never see another miracle? Is he worthy of praise? Of course he is. In Acts 8, Simon the Sorcerer was impressed by the miracles that Peter was doing in Samaria. He approached Peter and tried to pay money for the Holy Spirit, because he was keen to practice this same *magic.* Peter was indignant, because God was indignant. He said,

May your money perish with you, because you thought you could buy the gift of God with money! You have no part or share in this ministry, because your heart is not right before God. Repent of this wickedness and pray to the Lord in the hope that he may forgive you for having such a thought in your heart. For I see that you are full of bitterness and captive to sin (Acts 8:20-23, ESV).

We love miracles because we love God more. We love miracles because the Bible is full of them. We see how God can use them to authenticate his message. It would be unfaithful of us not to want to see him move in this way, but we should never get more focused on miracles than we are on God, or even on our character in Christ.

That said, pray for miracles. Pray that God would move again in greater measure. Pray that he would use *you* to bring glory to his name, and to see many lost souls come to faith as they witness the reality of God and his great power over all things. God be with you.

PART II

CHAPTER 1

POSITIVE CHRISTIAN AFFIRMATIONS

Words are things, so the saying goes. What you speak over yourself and believe is more important than what other people say about you. If you love to complain, then you will only attract bad things. But if you speak positive things over your life, you will develop a positive mindset, and this, in turn, will cause you to see yourself and others in a positive light.

Today, positive affirmations have become a common mindset tool. Many people, including Christians, use affirmations to develop positive mindsets. We are often told to recite some words over our lives and see the difference they will make.

But you may be wondering what positive Christian affirmations are. Are they going to help you in your healing journey? Are they necessary, and should Christians be speaking spiritual affirmations over their lives? Will they speed up the process of manifestation of healing in your life?

Well, understand that positive affirmations are not magical formulas. They will not help you to get results overnight if you don't know what they are and how to use them correctly.

What are Positive Christian/ Spiritual Affirmations?

These are positive Bible-based words that people speak over their lives or situation. The word of God tells us to guard our heart for out of it come the issues of life *(Proverbs 4:23)*. One of the ways that you can guard your heart is by saying and thinking about things that are true and positive, and that is where spiritual affirmations come in.

Unlike other positive affirmations, Christian affirmations are based on the word of God. Yes, you can speak positive words over your life or situation, but speaking those words doesn't mean that they will come true. You need to speak out words that you know and believe are true.

The Bible is the true word of God. When you create Bible-based affirmations, you will have the assurance that whatever you are speaking will come true in your life because it is the truth. Remember, faith comes by hearing the word of God. When you speak bible-based affirmations over your body, faith will rise on the inside, and healing will manifest.

When you know the truth about something, you start to see that thing differently. Let's say you didn't know that you were healed by Jesus 2000 years ago. If you start speaking healing affirmation over your body, you will start to look at healing differently and start to see yourself healed as these words penetrate your heart.

You may be wondering, are positive Christian affirmations scriptural? Yes, they are because the Bible encourages us to focus on thoughts that are true, lovely, praiseworthy, noble, and excellent. We live in a fallen world. The enemy is continuously feeding our minds with negative thoughts. Christian affirmations will help you to counter all those negative thoughts. Why can't I just memorize scripture you may ask and rightly so.

Well, affirmations are not meant to replace the word of God. But if we are, to be honest, most of us struggle to remember scripture, especially the ones which are long. Affirmations tend to be easy and short sentences that are easy to memorize.

Positive Affirmations and Healing

The Bible says that as we think, so are we in this world, meaning that our thought life affects how we live. How you think determines your belief system, and this, in turn, determines how you live. Your thoughts will determine whether healing will manifest in your body or not.

Many people want to live a changed life, but unfortunately, they try to change themselves outside instead of doing it inside-out. Movies and TV dramas have made us believe that exercising, going to a new place, and changing our diet will help us to live healthy lives. While these practices are great and important, they only work for some time if you don't work on your heart. To experience true change, you need to work on your heart hence the need for positive healing affirmations.

When you focus on negative things, you end up being stressed and depressed, and this will harm your health. You will struggle to stand firm in the word and hold on to the faith when you're always depressed. Positive affirmations will keep you on track and help you to continue standing firm in the word of God until healing manifests in your body.

The Lord wants you well. But you cannot enjoy divine health if you do not believe that God wants you well. When you take time each day to speak positive healing affirmations over your body, you are able to work on your mind and to cause it to be in tune with what God says about your health. The more you speak this truth to your heart, the more they become real, and the more your faith rises.

Something important to note is that you may feel silly at first when speaking these affirmations over your life. You may also feel discouraged when you don't experience change immediately. But don't quit, keep speaking even if the enemy taunts you. Keep speaking until there is manifestation.

How to Create Effective Positive Spiritual Affirmations

As I have said before, not all positive affirmations work. Yes, you might be speaking bible-based words, but that does not mean they'll manifest in your life. How you write your affirmations matters. Instead of writing things, generally, you need to be very specific to your need, in this case, healing.

So how do you create effective positive spiritual affirmations?

Use Verses that Meet that Particular Need

God has given us many precious promises for every need, and that means that healing has its own promises in the Bible. You need to look for bible verses that are related to health and wholeness. Study and meditate on them until they become real in your life.

The same is true for affirmations. Before you write any of them down, you need to get bible verses that match that particular need. You should not get a Bible verse about financial breakthroughs when you need a healing miracle. Yes, some bible verses are general, but it is better to create affirmations that speak directly to your situation.

Personalize the Verse.

The reason you should create affirmations from bible verses is to personalize the verse so that it can speak directly to you.

For example, let's use the verse in 3 John 2 which says:

Dear friend, I pray that you may enjoy good health and that all may go well with you even as your soul is getting along well.

Now we need to personalize this so that it can be relatable to us. So we can turn it into something like this;

I am enjoying good health, and all is going well with me even as my soul is getting along well.

See how the positive affirmation feels more relatable as you speak it out loud? The more you speak this out daily, the easier it becomes for you to see yourself being in good health and other things going well with you as your soul gets well. Every time you read the Bible, you will see yourself becoming healthy because, through this affirmation, you will know that there is a great link between reading the word of God and enjoying good health.

If you cannot create affirmations for one reason or another, you don't have to worry. I have included some affirmations at the end of this book that you can speak over your situation.

How to Use Affirmations

Writing down affirmations and speaking them once or twice will not cause them to work. Remember, the idea is to change your mind. You need to align your thoughts with what the word of God says about healing.

Put in a Visible Place

Some people write affirmations on a book or paper and then forget about them. That is not the way it works. Your affirmations should be in a visible place so that you can access them easily and read them out loud. If you have written your affirmations in a book, make sure you put that book in a visible place so that you can easily access it. For example, you can place it on your nightstand. That way, you can recite them whenever you wake up and before you go to bed.

You can write them on a sticky note and place them on your dressing mirror or wall. Putting these affirmations in visible places will make it easy for you to read them out loud when you're dressing or during your devotional time.

Recite Affirmations Frequently

As I've already stated, you should not recite your affirmations once and then forget about them. It needs to be a continuous process until they become true to you and cause you to experience change on the inside. When starting, recite as much as you can until they become ingrained in your mind.

For example, you may have to recite them when you wake up, several times in the course of the day and before you go to bed. Now here is something you should know before you start speaking them out loud. There will be times you will struggle with doubt because the affirmations contradict what is happening to your physical body.

But remember, you are a spirit living in a human body. Those words that you're speaking are spirit and life because they are the word of God. No matter how you feel, do not quit speaking them out loud. After a few days or weeks, these words will become a part of you, and instead of being doubtful, you will start to feel good about yourself.

Believe they're True

The personal development world always says that you need to fake it till you make it. They will encourage you to act like those affirmations are real in your life until they become real. But there's one thing you need to remember. Christians walk by faith and not by sight, so you cannot fake it till you make it. The word of God cannot be faked because it is the truth. You need to be living in it even if outside circumstances do not align with what the Bible says.

Visualization

God has given us the gift of imagination so that we can use it to see his word in the spirit realm and birth it in the physical. Your imagination is a spiritual womb that holds the word of God, which is a seed and causes it to produce the results that God wants his word to produce in your life.

Use your imagination to visualize what the word of God says. For example, when it says by the stripes of Jesus, you are healed, see Jesus taking your disease on his back at the scourging post. See your body getting healed because of the stripes that fell on his back. You need to hold the picture of Jesus taking your sickness and disease on his body firmly in your imagination until it becomes the truth in your heart and causes you to experience healing. Remember, even though Jesus died two thousand years ago, God is not limited by time. He operates outside time, so what happened two thousand years ago applies to you today.

If you have received a bad report from the doctors, do not spend time thinking how you are going to die or how that disease is going to have adverse effects on your body. Instead, use that time to visualize yourself healthy. See yourself doing the things that you love to do and enjoying good health in your imagination as you recite your affirmations.

Why Christian affirmations fail

Ever had a Christian call positive affirmations bad, chances are they did not work out for them, and so they concluded that they are not good. Instead of jumping into the bandwagon, try to find out why they failed in the first place.

Here are a few reasons why Christian affirmations fail;

Doubt

Without faith, it is impossible to please God, so when you're reciting affirmations, you need to believe that they are true because they are actually based on the word of God. When you doubt an affirmation, it means that you're doubting what the Bible says about healing. In essence, you are calling the word of God void. But we are told God's word will not return to Him void. It accomplishes his purposes on earth *(Isaiah 55:11)*. So as you recite, these affirmations believe that they are true and that they will come to pass.

Inconsistency

As much as we would like affirmations to work, some of us do not recite them consistently. We may recite them one or two days and then set them aside for a month before we recite them again. Some of us start out with a lot of excitement but start being inconsistent soon after.

Look, this is not just about getting some verses in the Bible, turning them into affirmations, and speaking them out loud whenever you feel like. You need to be consistent so that you can see results.

Giving up too Quickly

Maybe you have been reciting your positive affirmations for three weeks now, but you don't see any results, so you decide to quit. You may have concluded that positive Christian affirmations do not work. Instead of giving up, continue standing firm, and speaking these words over your life until you begin to see results in your body.

Just the way a farmer plants and waits to reap a harvest that is the way you need to plant positive Christian affirmations in your heart. Plant affirmations by reciting them. Water and apply fertilizer by being consistent and believing. With time you're going to see a harvest. It may take you longer than you thought, but you should not give up.

If used correctly, affirmations will bring up the intended results. Create your affirmation from the word of God. That way, it will become easy to believe what you are speaking over your life because they will be based on the truth. When creating affirmations, you need to use the promises that meet your particular need.

Write your affirmations in a notebook or sticky note so that you can access them easily. Remember to recite them consistently and believe that they will come true in your life. Don't give up quickly, and remember to use your imagination to visualize healing in your body.

Understand that affirmations should not replace the word of God. We should continue studying the word of God and allow it to transform us so that we can experience healing and wholeness.

CHAPTER 2

150 CHRISTIAN AFFIRMATIONS

In this chapter, we shall be looking at one hundred and fifty affirmations. I created these affirmations from Bible verses for reference and understanding.

1. God's power works best in my weakness

And he said unto me, My grace is sufficient for thee: for my strength is made perfect in weakness. Most gladly therefore will I rather glory in my infirmities, that the power of Christ may rest upon me.

2 Corinthians 12:9

2. Because I place my hope in the lord, my strength is renewed.

Isaiah 40:31 *- But they that wait upon the Lord shall renew their strength; they shall mount up with wings as eagles; they shall run, and not be weary; and they shall walk, and not faint.*

3. As I lose my life for Jesus sake, I find It

Matthew 10:39 *- Whoever finds their life lose it, and whoever loses their life for my sake will find it.*

4. God is able to do immeasurably more in my life than I could ever imagine.

Ephesians 3:20 *- Now to him who is able to do immeasurably more than all we ask or imagine, according to his power that is at work within us.*

5. I live by faith, not by sight.

2 Corinthians 12:7 *- Or because of these surpassingly great revelations. Therefore, in order to keep me from becoming conceited, I was given a thorn in my flesh, a messenger of Satan, to torment me.*

6. Because I believe in God and in Jesus, trouble leaves my heart.

John 14:1*- "Don't let your hearts be troubled. Believe in God, believe also in me.*

7. My faith makes me whole in spirit, soul and body.

Mark 5:34*- He told her, "Daughter, your faith has made you well. Go in peace and be healed from your illness."*

8. Because Jesus died for my sins, I am no longer separated from God. I live in close union with him.

Romans 5:10- *For if, while we were enemies, we were reconciled to God through the death of his Son, how much more, having been reconciled, will we be saved by his life!*

9. I love God's principles and meditate on them all day long.

Psalm 119:97- *How I love your instruction! Every day it is my meditation.*

10. Because I place my hope in God, I can soar like an eagle, run and not grow weary, walk and not be faint.

Isaiah 40:31-*But those who keep waiting for the LORD will renew their strength. Then they'll soar on wings like eagles; they'll run and not grow weary; they'll walk and not grow tired."*

11. I can see the Kingdom of God because I am born again.

John 3:3- Jesus replied, "Very truly I tell you, no one can see the kingdom of God unless they are born again."

12. I follow Jesus, no matter where he leads me.

Matthew 6:20 - *But store up for yourselves treasures in heaven, where moths and vermin do not destroy, and where thieves do not break in and steal*

13. I am being made holy by God's truths.

John 17:17 *- Sanctify them by the truth; your word is truth.*

14. I can approach God directly with freedom and confidence through faith in Jesus.

Ephesians 3:12*-In him and through faith in him we may approach God with freedom and Confidence.*

15. I worship the Lord my God and serve only him.

Luke 4:8*- Jesus answered, "It is written: 'Worship the Lord your God and serve him only."*

16. The "fullness of God" is available to me because I am deeply rooted in the love of Jesus.

Ephesians 3:17-19 - So that Christ may dwell in your hearts through faith. And I pray that you, being rooted and established in love, may have power, together with all the Lord's holy people, to grasp how wide and long and high and deep is the love of Christ, and to know this love that surpasses knowledge--that you may be filled to the measure of all the fullness of God.

17. As I give up control, release my life God and allow Jesus to live through me, God-sized things happen.

Galatians 2:20-*I have been crucified with Christ and I no longer live, but Christ lives in me. The life I now live in the body, I live by faith in the Son of God, who loved me and gave himself for me.*

18. I do not live by bread alone, but by every word that proceeds from the mouth of God.

Matthew 4:4-*Jesus answered, "It is written: 'Man shall not live on bread alone, but on every word that comes from the mouth of God."*

19. God pours out his love into my heart by the Holy Spirit.

Romans 5:5-*And hope does not put us to shame, because God's love has been poured out into our hearts through the Holy Spirit, who has been given to us.*

20. My life is bringing honour to Christ. God likes this.

Philippians 1:20- I eagerly expect and hope that I will in no way be ashamed but will have sufficient courage so that now as always Christ will be exalted in my body, whether by life or by death.

21. I can see the Kingdom of God because I am born again.

John 3:3- *Jesus replied, "Very truly I tell you, no one can see the kingdom of God unless they are born again."*

22. I don't worry about everyday life. God knows my needs and meets them because I make His Kingdom my primary concern.

Matthew 6:25-33 - *"Therefore I tell you, do not worry about your life, what you will eat or drink; or about your body, what you will wear. Is not life more than food, and the body more than clothes?*

Look at the birds of the air; they do not sow or reap or store away in barns, and yet your heavenly Father feeds them. Are you not much more valuable than they?

But seek first his kingdom and his righteousness, and all these things will be given to you as well.

23. God’s power works best in my weakness.

But he said to me, “My grace is sufficient for you, for my power is made perfect in weakness. Therefore, I will boast all the more gladly about my weaknesses, so that Christ's power may rest on me.”
2 Corinthians 12:9

24. Through the energy of Christ working powerfully in me, I teach others His truths.

To this end I strenuously contend with all the energy Christ so powerfully works in me.
Colossians 1:29

25. Because I fear the Lord and shun evil, my body is healthy, and my bones are nourished.

Do not be wise in your own eyes; fear the LORD and shun evil.
This will bring health to your body and nourishment to your bones.
Proverbs 3:7-8

26. I have been saved, not by works, but grace, so that I might do good works.

Not by works, so that no one can boast. For we are God's handiwork, created in Christ Jesus to do good works, which God prepared in advance for us to do.

Ephesians 2:9-10

27. My faith makes me whole in spirit, soul and body.

He said to her, "Daughter, your faith has healed you. Go in peace and be freed from your suffering."

Mark 5:34

28. When I call out to God, He answers me. He tells me things I wouldn't know otherwise.

Call to me and I will answer you and tell you great and unsearchable things you do not know.

Jeremiah 33:3

29. Because I place my hope in the Lord my strength is renewed.

but those who hope in the LORD will renew their strength. They will soar on wings like eagles; they will run and not grow weary; they will walk and not be faint.

Isaiah 40:31

30. As I follow Jesus…as I walk with him, I have peace.

"While they were still talking about this, Jesus himself stood among them and said to them, "Peace be with you."

Luke 24:36

31. I am open to miracles

"Who does great and unsearchable things, Wonders without number."

Job 5: 9

32. My Prayers are always answered

"I prayed to the LORD, and he answered me. He freed me from all my fears"
Psalm 34: 4

33. I Pay Attention to My Thoughts

"Finally, brothers and sisters, whatever is true, whatever is noble, whatever is right, whatever is pure, whatever is lovely, whatever is admirable—if anything is excellent or praiseworthy—think about such things"- **Philippians 4: 8**

34. I welcome miracles into my life

"Behold, I and the children whom the LORD has given me are for signs and wonders in Israel from the LORD of hosts, who dwells on Mount Zion"
Isaiah 8: 18

35. Through Faith, all my goals & dreams are within my reach

"May he give you the desire of your heart and make all your plans succeed"
Psalm 20: 4

36. My God has the power to change my life

"For I know the plans I have for you," declares the LORD, "plans to prosper you and not to harm you, plans to give you hope and a future"
Jeremiah 29: 11

37. Today, I expect a miracle

"Jesus Christ is the same yesterday and today and forever"
Hebrews 13: 8

38. I rely on my faith in God to realise my dreams, while others may give up

"But as for you, be strong and do not give up, for your work will be rewarded"

2 Chronicles 15: 7

39. Miracles happen to me all the time

"You are the God who works wonders; you have made known your might among the peoples"

Psalm 77: 14

40. My life is filled with wonderful events and miracles

"He is the one you praise; he is your God, who performed for you those great and awesome wonders you saw with your own eyes"

Deuteronomy 10: 21

41. It is time to reach my goals

"Trust in the Lord with all your heart and lean not on your own understanding; in all your ways submit to him, and he will make your paths straight"

Proverbs 3: 6

42. I am dedicated to making my Lord's desires a reality

"Take delight in the Lord, and he will give you the desires of your heart"

Psalm 37: 4

43. I am living a blessed life where my dreams are turning into reality every day

"Blessed be the Lord, Who daily loads us with benefits, The God of our salvation!"

Psalm 68: 19

44. Something wonderful is going to happen today

"Surely there is a future, and your hope will not be cut off"

Proverbs 23: 18

45. Today I find good fortunes wherever I go

"Blessed shall you be when you come in, and blessed shall you be when you go out"

Deuteronomy 28: 6

46. With prayers and God's guidance, my dreams will come true

"Trust in the LORD with all your heart and lean not on your own understanding; in all your ways submit to him, and he will make your paths straight"

Proverbs 3: 5 – 6

47. The sooner I start my dreams, the sooner they come true.

"The plans of the diligent lead to profit, as surely as hast leads to poverty"
Proverbs 21: 5

48. When I visualize my dreams come true, God makes it happen

"But we all, with unveiled face, beholding as in a mirror the glory of the Lord, are being transformed into the same image from glory to glory, just as by the Spirit of the Lord"
2 Corinthians 3: 18

49. I am committed to do everything to reach my goal through Jesus Christ

"I can do all things through Christ who gives me strength"
Philippians 4: 13

50. It is time to accept my good fortune.

"For you know the grace of our Lord Jesus Christ that though he was rich, yet for your sake he became poor, so that you through his poverty might become rich"

2 Corinthians 8: 9

51. I am ready to accept and receive miracles

"I am the Lord, the God of all mankind. Is anything too hard for me?"

Jeremiah 32: 27

52. I am open to miracles

"He replied, "Because you have so little faith. Truly I tell you, if you have faith as small as a mustard seed, you can say to this mountain, 'Move from here to there,' and it will move. Nothing will be impossible for you"

Matthew 17:20

53. I focus on my dreams in a gentle and relaxed manner, feeling ready for them to turn into reality.

"Commit to the Lord whatever you do, and he will establish your plans"

Proverbs 16: 3

54. New doors are opening all the time.

"Then I will set the key of the house of David on his shoulder,
When he opens no one will shut,
When he shuts no one will open"

Isaiah 22: 22

55. I now accept a wonderful, fulfilling career

"Sow your seed in the morning and do not be idle in the evening, for you do not know whether morning or evening sowing will succeed, or whether both of them alike will be good"

Ecclesiastes 11: 6

56. I feel fulfilled by all that I do

"May He grant you your heart's desire and fulfil all your counsel!"

Psalm 20: 4

57. As I create peace in my mind, my surrounding reflects this calm and peace

"Blessed are the peacemakers, for they shall be called sons of God"

Matthew 5: 9

58. Miracles happen every day

"If you can'?" said Jesus. "Everything is possible for one who believes"

Mark 9: 23

59. Everything is working for my highest good

"We know that all things work together for the good *of those who love God, who are called according to his purpose"*

Romans 8: 28

60. I am at peace with my life

"You keep him in perfect peace whose mind is stayed on you, because he trusts in you"

Isaiah 26: 3

61. I am more than willing to forgive all those who have harmed me

"Be kind to one another, tender-hearted, forgiving one another, as God in Christ forgave you"

Ephesians 4: 32

62. I take full responsibility for everything I do in my life.

"This day I call the heavens and the earth as witnesses against you that I have set before you life and death, blessings and curses. Now choose life, so that you and your children may live"

Deuteronomy 30: 19

63. I am one with the Lord who created me.

"But he who is joined to the Lord becomes one spirit with him"

1 Corinthians 6: 17

64. I am ready and willing to move forward, throwing away the sinful past, knowing God has forgiven me. I am free.

"Therefore, if anyone is in Christ, he is *a new creation; old things have passed away; behold, all things have become new"*

2 Corinthians 5: 17

65. I am happy and willing to release those that no longer serve me in my new life in Christ.

"Do not be yoked together with unbelievers. For what do righteousness and wickedness have in common? Or what fellowship can light have with darkness?"
2 Corinthians 6: 9

66. I am at peace with myself

"Peace I leave with you; my peace I give you. I do not give to you as the world gives. Do not let your hearts be troubled and do not be afraid"
John 14: 27

67. When I forgive and release my past, I walk into a new world of joy and happiness.

"Bear with each other and forgive one another if any of you has a grievance against someone. Forgive as the Lord forgave you"
Colossians 3: 13

68. I am ready and willing to enter the new world of wonderful and good experiences that are already coming my way

"If you are willing and obedient, you shall eat the good of the land"
Isaiah 1: 19

69. I voluntarily and happily release all negative thoughts, beliefs and concepts that no longer serve me

"When anxiety was great within me,
your consolation brought me joy"
Psalm 94: 19

70. Because I obey Jesus I remain in his love.

If you keep my commands, you will remain in my love, just as I have kept my Father's commands and remain in his love.
John 15:10

71. The cross of Christ is my power.

For Christ did not send me to baptize, but to preach the gospel--not with wisdom and eloquence, lest the cross of Christ be emptied of its power.
1 Corinthians 1:17

72. My God meets all my needs.

And my God will meet all your needs according to the riches of his glory in christ Jesus.
Philippians 4:19

73. God is my refuge and strength always ready to help me in times of trouble.

For the director of music. Of the Sons of Korah. According to alamoth. A song. God is our refuge and strength, an ever-present help in trouble.
Psalm 46:1

74. God gives me strength when I am weary and increases my power when I am weak.

He gives strength to the weary and increases the power of the weak.
Isaiah 40:29

75. Because I place my hope in God, I can soar like an eagle, run and not grow weary, walk and not be faint.

but those who hope in the LORD will renew their strength. They will soar on wings like eagles; they will run and not grow weary; they will walk and not be faint.
Isaiah 40:31

76. above, not earthly things. This gives me peace.

Since, then, you have been raised with Christ, set your hearts on things above, where Christ is, seated at the right hand of God. Set your minds on things above, not on earthly things.

Colossians 3:1-2

77. I guard my heart because it determines the course of my life.

Above all else, guard your heart, for everything you do flows from it.

Proverbs 4:23

78. I trust God at all times because he is my refuge.

Trust in him at all times, you people; pour out your hearts to him, for God is our refuge.

Psalm 62:8

79. AS I LOSE MY LIFE FOR JESUS' SAKE, I FIND IT

Whoever finds their life will lose it, and whoever loses their life for my sake will find it. ***Matthew 10:39***

80. God keeps me in perfect peace because I trust in Him and fix my thoughts on Him.

You will keep in perfect peace those whose minds are steadfast, because they trust in you.
Isaiah 26:3

81. I am open to miracles

"If you can'?" said Jesus. "Everything is possible for one who believes."
Mark 9:23

82. My prayers are always answered

Therefore, I tell you, whatever you ask for in prayer, believe that you have received it, and it will be yours.

Mark 11:2

83. I pay attention to my thoughts

My son pay attention to what I say; turn your ear to my words.

Proverbs 4:20

84. I welcome miracles into my life

He is the one you praise; he is your God, who performed for you those great and awesome wonders you saw with your own eyes.

Deuteronomy 10:21

85. Through Faith, all my goals & dreams are within my reach

Trust in the LORD with all thine heart; and lean not unto thine own understanding. In all thy ways acknowledge him, and he shall direct thy paths.
Proverbs 3:5-6

86. My God has the power to change my life

Therefore, if anyone is in Christ, the new creation has come: The old has gone, the new is here!
2 Corinthians 5:17

87. Today, I expect a miracle

He replied, "Because you have so little faith. Truly I tell you, if you have faith as small as a mustard seed, you can say to this mountain, 'Move from here to there,' and it will move. Nothing will be impossible for you."
Matthew 17:20

88. I rely on my faith in God to realise my dreams, while others may give up

For I know the plans I have for you," declares the Lord, "plans to prosper you and not to harm you, plans to give you hope and a future.

Jeremiah 29:11

89. Miracles happen to me all the time

And Jesus said to him, "'If you can'! All things are possible for one who believes."'

Mark 9:23

90. My life is filled with wonderful events & miracles

Now to him who is able to do immeasurably more than all we ask or imagine, according to his power that is at work within us,

Ephesians 3:20

91. It is time to reach my goals

"Brothers and sisters, I do not consider myself yet to have taken hold of it. But one thing I do: Forgetting what is behind and straining toward what is ahead, I press on toward the goal to win the prize for which God has called me heavenward in Christ Jesus."

Philippians 3:13-14

92. I am dedicated to making my Lord's desires a reality

I delight to do Your will, O my God;
Your Law is within my heart."

Psalm 40:8

93. I am living a blessed life where my dreams are turning into reality every day

"But blessed is the one who trusts in the LORD, whose confidence is in him.
They will be like a tree planted by the water that sends out its roots by the stream. It does not fear when heat comes; its leaves are always green. It has no worries in a year of drought and never fails to bear fruit."

Jeremiah 17: 7-8

94. SOMETHING WONDERFUL IS GOING TO HAPPEN TODAY

"But if I were you, I would appeal to God; I would lay my cause before him.
He performs wonders that cannot be fathomed, miracles that cannot be counted.

Job 5:8-9

95. Today I find good fortunes wherever I go

"I can do all things through Christ who gives me strength."

Philippians 4:13

96. With prayers & God's guidance, my dreams will come true

"Commit to the Lord whatever you do, and he will establish your plans. "

Proverbs 16:3

97. The sooner I start my dreams, the sooner they come true.

"So, do not throw away your confidence; it will be richly rewarded. You need to persevere so that when you have done the will of God, you will receive what he has promised."

Hebrews 10:35-36

98. When I visualize my dreams come true, God makes it happen

For I know the plans I have for you, declares the Lord, plans for welfare and not for evil, to give you a future and a hope. Then you will call upon me and come and pray to me, and I will hear you. You will seek me and find me, when you seek me with all your heart.

Jeremiah 29:11-13

99. I am committed to do everything to reach my goal through Jesus Christ

"Commit to the Lord whatever you do, and he will establish your plans. "

Proverbs 16:3

100. It is time to accept my good fortune.

"In their hearts humans plan their course, but the Lord establishes their steps."

Proverbs 16:9

101. I am ready to accept & receive miracles

You are the God who works wonders;
You have made known Your strength among the peoples.

Psalm 77:14

102. I am open to miracles

"'If you can'?" said Jesus. "Everything is possible for one who believes."

Mark 9:23

103. I focus on my dreams in a gentle and relaxed manner, feeling ready for them to turn into reality.

I press on toward the goal for the prize of the upward call of God in Christ Jesus.

Philippians 3:14

104. New doors are opening all the time.

"'I know your works. Behold, I have set before you an open door, which no one is able to shut. I know that you have but little power, and yet you have kept my word and have not denied my name.

Revelation 3:8

105. I now accept a wonderful, fulfilling career

Many are the plans in the mind of a man, but it is the purpose of the Lord that will stand.

Proverbs 19:21

106. I feel fulfilled by all that I do

Being confident of this, that he who began a good work in you will carry it on to completion until the day of Christ Jesus.

Philippians 1:6

107. As I create peace in my mind, my surrounding reflects this calm and peace

"Therefore, since we have been justified by faith, we have peace with God through our Lord Jesus Christ. Through him we have also obtained access by faith into this grace in which we stand, and we rejoice in hope of the glory of God."

Romans 5: 1-2

108. Miracles happen every day

You are the God who works wonders; you have made known your might among the peoples.

Psalm 77:14

109. Everything is working for my highest good

And we know that in all things God works for the good of those who love him, who have been called according to his purpose.

Romans 8:28

110. I am at peace with my life

"Do not be anxious about anything, but in everything by prayer and supplication with thanksgiving let your requests be made known to God. And the peace of God, which surpasses all understanding, will guard your hearts and your minds in Christ Jesus."

Philippians 4:6-7

111. I am more than willing to forgive all those who have harmed me

"And whenever you stand praying, forgive, if you have anything against anyone, so that your Father also who is in heaven may forgive you your trespasses."

Mark 11:25

112. I am one with the Lord who created me.

For I am the Lord your God, who holds your right hand, who says to you," Do not fear, I will help you."

Isaiah 41:13

113. I am ready and willing to move forward, throwing away the sinful past, knowing God has forgiven me. I am free.

"Forget the former things; do not dwell on the past. See, I am doing a new thing! Now it springs up; do you not perceive it? I am making a way in the wilderness and streams in the wasteland.

Isaiah 43:18-19

114. I am happy and willing to release those that no longer serve me in my new life in Christ.

Brothers and sisters, I do not consider myself yet to have taken hold of it. But one thing I do: Forgetting what is behind and straining toward what is ahead, I press on toward the goal to win the prize for which God has called me heavenward in Christ Jesus.

Philippians 3:13-14

115. I am at peace with myself

“Great peace have those who love your law; nothing can make them stumble.”

Psalm 119:165

116. When I forgive and release my past, I walk into a new world of joy and happiness.

"Let all bitterness and wrath and anger and clamor and slander be put away from you, along with all malice. Be kind to one another, tenderhearted, forgiving one another, as God in Christ forgave you."

Ephesians 4:31-32

117. I am ready and willing to enter the new world of wonderful and good experiences that are already coming my way

But those who hope in the LORD will renew their strength. They will soar on wings like eagles; they will run and not grow weary, they will walk and not be faint.

Isaiah 40:31

118. I voluntarily and happily release all negative thoughts, beliefs and concepts that no longer serve me

Instead, let the Spirit renew your thoughts and attitudes. Put on your new nature, created to be like God–truly righteous and holy.

Ephesians 4:23-24

119. I am a child of the King.

1 Peter 2:9 *-But you are God's chosen treasure—priests who are kings, a spiritual "nation" set apart as God's devoted ones. He called you out of darkness to experience his marvellous light, and now he claims you as his very own. He did this so that you would broadcast his glorious wonders throughout the world.*

120. I am wonderfully & remarkably made.

Psalm 139:14– *I will praise You because I have been remarkably and wonderfully made. Your works are wonderful, and I know this very well.*

121. I am worth more than the most precious stones.

Proverbs 31:10 – *A good woman is hard to find and worth far more than diamonds.*

_122._ I know that I am more than a conqueror.

Romans 8:31 – *If God is for us, who can be against us? We are more than conquerors through Him who loves us)*

123. I am strong and courageous & no evil shall touch me.

Deuteronomy 31:6 NIV – *Be strong and courageous. Do not be afraid or terrified because of them, for the LORD your God goes with you; he will never leave you nor forsake you.*

124. I am not who I once was for my sins are forgiven. Indeed, I am a new creation

2 Corinthians 5:17 – *Therefore if anyone is in Christ, he is a new creature; the old things passed away; behold, new things have come.*

125. I believe with all my heart that my prayers are heard and Are Being brought to pass.

Mark 11:24 *– I tell you, you can pray for anything, and if you believe that you've received it, it will be yours.*

126. I will boldly & unashamedly live for God, not man.

Philippians 1:20 *– I eagerly expect and hope that I will have nothing to be ashamed of. I will speak very boldly and honour Christ in my body, now as always, whether I live or die.*

127. I cannot be led astray for God is always guiding me.

Psalm 71:17 *– O God, you have taught me ever since I was young, and I still talk about the miracles you have done.*

128. I will always seek first my Lord's kingdom and His righteousness.

Matthew 6:33 – *Seek the Kingdom of God above all else, and live righteously, and he will give you everything you need.*

129. I am delighted to be the light of Christ; I shine wherever I go. (Matthew 5:13-16)

Psalm 71:17 *– O God, you have taught me ever since I was young, and I still talk about the miracles you have done.*

130. My Lord covers me with His feathers so that I am assured of refuge under His wings.

Psalm 91:4 *– He will cover you with his feathers. He will shelter you with his wings. His faithful promises are your armour and protection.*

131. My Lord's wisdom exceeds all things, that worldly knowledge cannot compete. I will not depend on my own understanding

Proverbs 3:5 *– Trust in the LORD with all your heart; do not depend on your own understanding.*

132. Through the spiritual nature, I can express love, joy, peace, patience, kindness, goodness, faithfulness, gentleness, and self-control.

Galatians 5:22-23 – *But the spiritual nature produces love, joy, peace, patience, kindness, goodness, faithfulness, gentleness, and self-control. There are no laws against things like that.*

133. I know & declare that no matter what I go through, God's glory will be revealed through my life.

Romans 8:18 – *I consider that the sufferings of this present time are not worthy to be compared with the glory that is to be revealed to me.*

Philippians 1:6 – *I'm convinced that God, who began this good work in you, will carry it through to completion on the day of Christ Jesus.*

134. My Lord's mercy ensures that all things are working for my good.

Romans 8:28 *– God causes all things to work together for good to those who love God, to those who are called according to His purpose.*

135. God has promised victory for me and not punishment. I declare that right now He is fighting on my behalf.

Deuteronomy 20:4 *– For the Lord your God is going with you! He will fight for you against your enemies, and he will give you victory!*

136. I have a future filled with hope & prosperity for a brighter future.

Jeremiah 29:11 *– For I know the plans I have for you," declares the Lord, "plans to prosper you and not to harm you, plans to give you hope and a future.*

137. I have all that I need to do well in life.

2 Peter 1:3 *– By his divine power, God has given us everything we need for living a godly life. We have received all of this by coming to know him, the one who called us to himself by means of his marvellous glory and excellence.*

138. No Fear can hold me down.

2 Timothy 1:7 *– For God has not given us a spirit of fear and timidity, but of power, love, and self-discipline*

139. I have peace that surpasses all understanding.

Philippians 4:6-8 *– Don't worry about anything; instead, pray about everything. Tell God what you need and thank him for all he has done. Then you will experience God's peace, which exceeds anything we can understand. His peace will guard your hearts and minds as you live in Christ Jesus.*

140. I WILL ALWAYS BE ALERT & PERSISTANT To Help All Believers

Ephesians 6:18*- Pray in the Spirit at all times and on every occasion. Stay alert and be persistent in your prayers for all believers everywhere.*

141. I can overcome anything & everything with Christ.

1 Corinthians 15:57 *New Living Translation (NLT) - But thank God! He gives us victory over sin and death through our Lord Jesus Christ.*

142. Go, Let your will be done.

Matthew 6:10– Thy kingdom come, Thy will be done in earth, as it is in heaven.

Exodus 15:26

143. The Lord restores me to health and heals my wounds

Jeremiah 30:17 *The fact that the Lord restores you to health indicates that health is your natural state. When you get a wound, what does it do? It heals! In your natural state you are healthy and whole. The Lord brings you back to that place.*

144. By his wounds I am healed

Isaiah 53:5 *In a very poetic turn of phrase, Isaiah brilliantly demonstrates that our healing – whether it be physical or spiritual – begins with the healing work of Jesus. Jesus was a healer, and it is through his redemptive work on the cross that we can begin to understand what healing is and experience it to the depths of our being.*

145. The Lord heals all my diseases

Psalm 103:3 *No matter what is causing you dis-ease, to not be at ease, the Lord heals it* ALL. *He's not just interested in your spiritual condition*

. He demonstrated that through Jesus when he went around healing every disease and sickness ***Matthew 4:23.***

146. God strengthens and upholds me

Isaiah 41:10 *God is like a magical elixir and crutch. He does whatever he needs to do to get you back up on your feet. He's there every step of the way, and he knows sometimes those steps can be difficult.*

147. I use wise words to speak healing

Proverbs 12:18 *You can do your part in helping yourself and others heal by speaking words of healing rather than dwelling on illness and disease. Instead of saying, "I'm sick", you can say words like, "I feel like my body is fighting off something." Your words can bring healing to your own physical body and to your relationships as well!*

148. A joyful heart is good medicine

Proverbs 17:22 *You can do a lot to assist and speed your healing by focusing on being positive, fun and light hearted. It's more difficult to do when you're not feeling well, but it is possible. The human spirit can endure a sick body, but who can bear a crushed spirit?*

149. My faith makes me whole in spirit, soul and body.

Mark 5:34- *He told her, "Daughter, your faith has made you well. Go in peace and be healed from your illness."*

150. Because Jesus died for my sins, I am no longer separated from God. I live in close union with him.

For if, while we were enemies, we were reconciled to God through the death of his Son, how much more, having been reconciled, will we be saved by his life!
Romans 5:10

PART III

CHAPTER 1

FIFTEEN HEALING MIRACLE EXPERIENCES

01 Healing Is Your Right in Christ Jesus

There are so many Christian folks who are bedridden either in their homes or hospitals that should not be in the condition they are in. Their ignorance of Scriptures has kept them in that condition. The Lord Jesus Christ said, "...***You err, not knowing the Scriptures, nor the power of God***" Matthew 22: 29. The devil, through sicknesses, diseases, and other forms of infirmities, has beaten these Christians because they do not know that healing is their right in Christ Jesus.

When you study the Scriptures, you will find several Bible healing promises concerning you and your health. An example is in Luke 13: 16, where the Lord Jesus healed a woman. "***So, ought not this woman, being a daughter of Abraham, whom Satan has bound—think of it—for eighteen years, be loosed from this bond on the Sabbath?***" As an heir of Papa Abraham and joint-heir with Christ, healing and living in divine health are your birthright in

Christ Jesus. No circumstance, sin, or person can inhibit you from getting your healing miracles because you are born of God.

Sometime in June 2015, Osaro Agbe male 19, and two of his friends attacked a local church pastor while trying to break into his church on a rainy day. Osaro's parents are deacon and deaconess in their church in Benin City. All their four children were born and raised in their church, and their parents ensured that their children were given a good Christian upbringing. In fact, the other three children are what you would call Christian children because of the way they carried themselves. Osaro was like his siblings until he went to the University in another state, unlike his siblings, who all schooled in Ekpoma, a close-by town to Benin City where they were born.

Osaro obviously joined a cult in school, and his parents never knew about it until the day Osaro, together with occult friends, broke into a church, stole, and attacked the pastor. About two weeks after the incident, Osaro woke up one morning without his senses. He could not talk coherently, and he became violent. In a few weeks' time, he became obese, and a foul smell emanated from his mouth when he tried to talk. His parent took him to several hospitals, but nothing could be done for him. He could not return to university and remained at home for over four years.

In January 2020, the new pastor posted to Osaro's parents' church came to visit them unannounced. He saw the condition that the family was in because of Osaro. After praying with them, he told them the problem was as a result of Osaro's attack on a pastor. The parents suddenly connected Osaro's plight to what he did over four years ago. Accompanied by their pastor, they went to the church that Osaro and his friends had attacked the pastor. They apologized to the pastor, and he prayed for Osaro, saying, "Osaro, I forgive you, and in the name of Jesus, I command the devil of darkness to come out of you!" Instantly, Osaro was restored, and He was healed. Praise God!

Do not allow the devil to rob you of your healing. Pray to God for your healing, and He will heal you. He loves you and wants you well.

Prayer

Blessed Father, I thank You for the eternal life You have given me. I thank You because healing is my birthright in Christ Jesus. Your Word says healings are Your children's bread. Therefore, I declare that I receive healing today – I am completely made whole, in Jesus' Name. Amen.

02 Healing Is from Above

Sometimes we find people wondering whether they can actually get healed. They think that their sicknesses or ordeals are too big for God to handle. The Word of God asks, "***Behold, I am the LORD, the God of all flesh. Is anything too hard for me?***" Jeremiah 32: 27. No matter how serious your health challenge might be, the Lord Jesus Christ said, "...***With man it is impossible, but not with God. For all things are possible with God,***" Mark 10: 27.

The Scriptures are filled with several Bible healing promises to stir your faith so that you can receive your healing miracles. God can use any means to heal you; be it scientific or spiritual healing, know that anything is possible with God. What you need to do to get healed is to pray to God for healing. Remember how Hezekiah was sick to death, and Prophet Isaiah even conveyed God's message that he would die, but he prayed, and God healed him and added to his years. "***Go and tell Hezekiah that this is what the LORD, the God of your father David, says: 'I have heard your prayer; I have seen your tears. Behold, I will add fifteen years to your life,***" Isaiah 38: 5. Healing is not manmade but from heaven above. God delights in seeing you living in divine health. He is still in the business of healing His children.

To every mother who just gave birth, the joy and excitement of giving birth and seeing your new baby is usually inexplicable. That was the case of Gertrude N'zolo, a 33 years mother of 3. But her joy was cut short a few minutes after giving birth to her third child. As she tried adjusting herself so she could carry her new bundle of joy, a doctor came into her ward and walked straight to her bedside. "Congratulations, ma." The doctor said as he stared at her and her baby. "Please, I need to personally inform you that there is a problem." The doctor began. Gertrude was at a loss at what the doctor was talking about because her pregnancy was normal, and she delivered her son with no issues. "During delivery, we observed what looks like cervical cancer, but we need to carry out further testing to be really sure," the doctor concluded. Gertrude turned to look at her husband, who was there all along but said very few words. The look on his face confirmed to her that he has already been informed about the discovery.

After a smear test was done, it was confirmed that Gertrude had cervical cancer. The situation was, in fact, far more severe than the doctors suspected, and Gertrude was facing imminent death. She had to return to the hospital. According to Gertrude, her mind was constantly filled with thoughts of death. She could not walk long distances as she would always feel a terrible pain in her lower abdomen and legs. As with cervical cancer patients, she started experiencing severe discharges from her vagina. The cancer was fast spreading. As her health deteriorated, she had to stop working.

One beautiful day, as she sat in her living room watching television, she saw a church program where a popular pastor was healing sick folks. She immediately copied the church address and went to that church the following Sunday. After a few counseling classes, she met with the pastor of the church who readily prayed for her. As he prayed, she instantly felt a change was happening. After a fortnight, the symptoms all disappeared. She went to see her doctors, and they were so surprised to see her totally transformed. They did several tests on her, but there was no trace of cervical cancer in her body. She was cancer-free! Glory to God!

Prayer

Father God, I thank You for Your healing power at work in the Body of Christ today. I thank You because Your healing power can surge through to heal any form of infirmity. I declare Your healing power over my body, and in the Name of the Lord Jesus Christ, I receive healing right now. Amen.

03 How to Receive Your Healing

Unlike what some Christians think, receiving healing or miracles is as easy as receiving salvation. Many of us have been taught or made to believe that receiving miracles is hard and complicated, like rocket science. No, that is not true at all. From what we read in the scriptures, faith is the ingredient required to receive healing, just like salvation. All the people the Lord Jesus Christ healed in the Bible demonstrated their faith to receive their healing. A government official who wanted the Lord to heal his son, who was sick in Capernaum, came pleading to get his son healed. ***"Go," said Jesus. "Your son will live." The man took Jesus at His word and departed.*** " John 4: 50.

Also, in Capernaum, a centurion came to the Lord to receive healing for his servant, who was seriously ill. When the Lord saw his faith, "***Then Jesus said to the centurion, "Go your way; and as you have believed, so let it be done for you." And his servant was healed that same hour***" Matthew 8: 13.

The two blind men who besought the Lord for their sights to be restored are yet another example. "***Then He touched their eyes and said, "According to your faith, will it be done to you,***" Matthew 9: 29.

The woman with the issue of blood for twelve long years also demonstrated her faith for healing. ***Jesus turned and saw her, " Take courage, daughter," He said, "your faith has healed you."***

And the woman was cured from that very hour, Matthew 9: 22. These are very few examples of how you can demonstrate your faith to receive your healing.

When Rachel got married three years ago, she was full of great expectations of a happy family with her husband and the beautiful children she felt the Lord would surely bless them with. And that was her hope from the wedding day until her delivery date. Everything looked normal till her due date when labor lasted for about two days. The midwife and the other nurses at the community health center where she registered and attended her antenatal clinics tried to help her bring the baby out. Although it was her first delivery, the midwife and nurses were experienced, but all their efforts that day seemed as though they were greenhorns.

In the process of trying to help the baby out, one of the nurses forcefully pulled her baby's hand. The baby came out, but after a few days, Rachel discovered that her son could not move his left hand. She rushed to the hospital, and she was told that the baby's hand was pulled out of his shoulder; hence he cannot use the hand. Her baby had to grow up deformed in his left hand. This disheartened the young family. The doctors advised her to get physiotherapy to help the baby move and use his hand, but for more than a year, nothing seemed to change.

One day while Rachel was shopping, the owner of the shop, a Spirit-filled Christian, and his wife saw the condition of Great, Rachel's little boy, and they prayed with her and encouraged her to continue with the physiotherapy. They also advised Rachel to proclaim God's Word for complete healing over his hand as many times as she could each day. Her faith was stirred up, and for the next three months, Rachel did what the couple told her. She proclaimed God's healing promises from the Bible while she continued with the physiotherapy. On the tenth of June 2020, little Great woke up and started to use both hands. The whole family and their neighbors were thrown into great jubilation. This is a case of both scientific and spiritual healing. Praise God forevermore!

Prayer

Precious Father, the entrance of Your Word brings light. I thank You for the illumination Your Word has brought to me today. I declare that my faith is alive and active to receive the miracles and healings I desire in the Name of the Lord, Jesus Christ. Amen.

04 Power In The Name Of Jesus Christ

The Word of God says, ***"Therefore God also has highly exalted Him and given Him the name which is above every name, that at the name of Jesus every knee should bow, of those in heaven, and of those on earth, and of those under the earth, and that every tongue should confess that Jesus Christ is Lord, to the glory of God the Father"*** Philippians 2: 9 – 11. By implication of these verses, anything that is named or can be described in heaven, on earth, and under the earth is subject to the Name of the Lord Jesus Christ. Everything that exists in heaven, on earth or under the earth in physical or spiritual form is subject to the Name of Jesus Christ.

What is that thing that ails you; does it have a name? In what location does it exist? Whatever it is, whether you know the name or you cannot describe it, the Name of Jesus Christ is superior to it. At the gate called Beautiful, Apostles Peter and John demonstrated that the Name of Jesus Christ has power over paralysis. "***But Peter said, "I have no silver and gold, but what I do have I give to you. In the name of Jesus Christ of Nazareth, rise up and walk,***" Acts 3: 6.

The Apostle Paul, by revelation, said these about the Lord Jesus Christ. "***For by him, all things were created, in heaven and on earth, visible and invisible, whether thrones or dominions or rulers or authorities—all things were created through him and for him***" Colossians 1: 16. "***And he put all things under his feet and gave him as head over all things to the church.***" Ephesians

1: 22. If you have the knowledge and understanding, no sickness or affliction can successfully fasten itself on your body.

The joy of every footballer is to be free of injuries, able to play for his club regularly, and win laurels. These were Solomon Okao's dream as he played for one of the clubs in Nigeria's Premier League. As an attacking midfielder, he must always be able to assist the strikers in scoring goals and even scoring himself. On a particular day, while his team was playing an away match, Solomon fell as he was tackled by an opposing defender. What seemed like a small fall aggravated to the point that Solomon could not play for his team again. He could barely stand by himself, let alone walk. He felt excruciating pains from his waistline down to his ankles anytime he tried to take a few steps. He had to use a wheelchair for more than two years.

Solomon's younger brother Allen took him to different hospitals and specialists after his team doctors could not do anything for him anymore. There was no clear diagnosis for his case. In fact, one of the doctors at his football club told him his problem was spiritual as it has defied all medical treatments. Solomon remained in this state for over two years until a family friend visited him and led him to Christ and invited him to church.

For another six months, Allen wheeled Solomon to the church where he heard God's Word, and his faith grew. He started claiming healing promises from the bible daily. On a particular midweek service in January 2018, while Solomon was in church enjoying the cooperate anointing from the service, his pastor walked up to him and said, 'Brother Solomon, this wheelchair is not God's will for you. In the Name of Jesus Christ, stand up!' By faith, Solomon stood, and the anointing overwhelmed him. He fell on the floor, and when he got up, he started jumping and running. He was totally healed!

Prayer

Father, I thank You for the awesome power in the Name of Jesus Christ. You have highly exalted that Name and brought everything, name, person or circumstances under the subjection of the Name of Jesus Christ. I thank You Lord God and I bring every situation around me to the subjection of that powerful Name. Amen.

05 You Have Authority Over Sickness

Every Christian has authority over any sickness, infirmity, disease, or affliction. He can lay hands on the sick and command the sickness to depart. He can cast out the devil or demons responsible for any sickness or affliction because the authority the Lord Jesus Christ had while on earth has been transferred to him. The Lord gave you the power to "***Heal the sick, raise the dead, cleanse those with leprosy, and drive out demons. Freely you received, freely give***" Matthew 10: 8.

The disciples of Jesus Christ demonstrated tremendous authority over sickness and devils. For example, the Apostle Peter, "***As a result, people brought the sick into the streets and laid them on cots and mats, so that at least Peter's shadow might fall on some of them as he passed by. Crowds gathered also from the towns around Jerusalem, bringing their sick and those tormented by impure spirits, and all of them were healed***" Acts 5: 15 – 16. Can you see that? Apostle, Peter, did not even pray, but the anointing was in his shadow to heal the sick.

The Apostle Paul's ministry was also characterized by great healing miracles. "***People even took handkerchiefs and aprons that had touched Paul's body, and they carried them to everyone who was sick. All of the sick people were healed, and the evil spirits went out,***" Acts 19: 12. Several other disciples in the Bible performed healings, signs, and wonders just as the Lord said we will do. "***I tell you the truth, anyone who believes in me will do***

the same works I have done, and even greater works, because I am going to be with the Father" John 14: 12.

Here is a testimony of Mike Ogbebor:

"There was a time I wouldn't dare eat any food once it was past 8pm in the evening. I remember, on several occasions, how I was rushed to the hospital for eating candies, chocolates, or even a bite of biscuits when I was in primary and secondary schools. I grew up to know that I do not taste any food from 8pm. How this came about I do not know. On many occasions, I asked my mum, but all she could say is that *'you are just like that. All the doctors and hospitals I took to said nothing was wrong with you'*. Throughout my university days, my friends wondered why I would not taste anything except water after 8pm. I could only tell one or two friends that were really close to me. Even when I got married, my wife had to adjust to my eating pattern. On a particular occasion, my wife persuaded me to eat little rice because we got home late and had not eaten any food all day. I hesitated but later ate little. Ten minutes later, my stomach was burning like hell, and I ended up in the hospital that night.

On our second wedding anniversary, my mother-in-law invited my wife and me to her church for our anniversary thanksgiving. Though I was not cut out for such things, out of respect, I obliged and attended. I got born again in that service and started attending church regularly and studying my Bible. As I studied, I read about the healing miracles and other Bible healing promises. I discovered that I have authority over the devil and sicknesses. So, I started to pray to God for healing.

I grew my faith with God's Word and speaking in tongues. I set December 25th, 2019, Charismas Day, as my date of healing. On that day, I deliberately ate at 8:30pm. After eating, I went to my room to start praying fervently in other tongues, waiting for the devil to show up. Four minutes had not even passed when I started feeling the pains around my stomach region. This time, I told myself that it was time that I dealt with the devil. This pain continued. The more the pain continued, the fiercer I prayed in tongues. I prayed till about 12 am, and though I noticed the pain was gone. I refused to stop praying because I did not want the devil to play pranks on me. I prayed till 4am before I went to sleep. Since that day till now, the devil never came back, and I can eat anytime I feel like. In fact, I have biscuits that I eat from 8pm to shame the devil. I am completely free now. Praise God!

Prayer

I thank You, Father, for giving me power over the devil, sicknesses and all infirmities. By the authority I have in the Name of Jesus Christ, I declare that no sickness or disease can fasten itself or survive in my body. I paralyze their effects on my body in the Name of the Lord Jesus Christ. Amen.

06 Connection between Sickness & Sin

A lot of sicknesses are caused by sin. A Christian can get afflicted with sickness or disease because of the sin he or she committed. The Psalmist affirms that one's health can be distorted because of the sin the person committed. "***There is no soundness in my flesh because of Your indignation; <u>there is no health in my bones because of my sin</u>***" Psalm 38: 3. Micah also revealed the mind of God concerning Israel in his time. "***So also I will make you sick, striking you down, desolating you because of your sins***" Micah 6: 13.

Once, the disciples of Jesus Christ asked Him the cause of a particular man's blindness. "***And His disciples asked Him, "Rabbi, who sinned, this man or his parents, that he would be born blind?***" John 9: 2. This infers that the disciples were aware that some sicknesses could be caused by sin. The Lord's response did not particularly rule out the possibilities of ailments being caused by sins committed by those that are sick. ""***Neither this man nor his parents sinned," said Jesus, "but this happened so that the works of God might be displayed in him***" John 9: 3.

Remember how Aaron and Miriam spoke against Moses and how Miriam was plagued with leprosy. This is an example of sickness resulting from sin. "***When the cloud lifted from above the tent, Miriam's skin was leprous—it became as white as snow. Aaron turned toward her and saw that she had a defiling skin disease, and he said to Moses, "Please, my lord, I ask you not***

to hold against us the sin we have so foolishly committed. Do not let her be like a stillborn infant coming from its mother's womb with its flesh half eaten away" Number 12: 10 – 12.

Marcella Joseph was born and raised as a Christian. Her parents are strong Catholics who do not take the disciplining of their five children lightly. Attending early morning Mass daily and observing other Catholic prayer rites was compulsory. So Marcella and her siblings, without questioning, practiced the religious rituals from childhood. However, as she turned 17, she started rebelling against some of her parents' strict decisions. One fateful day, in defiance to her parents' strict home training, she started flirting with some of the mass-servers. According to her, their pious dressing and walk during mass was what intrigued her to want to date as many of the mass-servers. Even when a particular man refused to give her attention, she persisted until she succeeded in 'defiling' him.

Marcella's desire to seduce men of God grew, and when she went to university, she continued. She carefully and skilfully selected her victims. Her preference was those that serve at the altar or those that work closely with them.

As she was about to graduate from the university, Marcella noticed she was unusually putting on weight. Her hitherto great figure soon vanished, and within weeks her legs became so swollen she could not move them. At first, Marcella thought she was pregnant, but after tests in the hospital, pregnancy was ruled out. At some point, the doctors thought her sickness was Edema, but that was also ruled out as she could not sleep either during the day or night. She consistently had nightmares and became restless.

Her parents, being devout Christians, knew her condition was a result of her terrible sins against God. So, they combined prayers and scientific solutions. When no hospital could help, especially with the nightmares, they resorted to carrying Marcella from one church or prayer house to another. God had mercy on Marcella. One day while watching a Faith and Miracle program on television, the pastor, through the Word of Knowledge, called out Marcella's case. The pastor asked her to confess her sins and sincerely repent. She did as the pastor said, and for the first time in months, Marcella slept well. Within the next two weeks, her swelling reduced. She was totally healed by the power of God. Halleluiah!

Prayer

In the Name of the Lord Jesus Christ, I declare that even if the prince of this world comes, he has nothing on me. Sin has no dominion over me. I am the righteousness of God in Christ Jesus. Thus, I am living the superior life in Christ. I declare no sickness or infirmity in my body. I thank You, Precious Father. Amen.

07 Real Miracles Today

Are you one of those who claim that there are no more miracles or healings in the world today or that miracles stopped with the Apostles? If you belong to that school of thought, you have been lied to by the devil because that is not what the Scriptures teach us. The Word of God says that "***Jesus Christ is the same yesterday and today and forever***" Hebrews 13: 8. The implication of that statement is that if He healed and performed miracles in Bible days, He is still doing the same today through us. Today, we are His outstretched hands of healing in our world. He said, "***And these signs will accompany those who believe: In My name they will drive out demons; they will speak in new tongues; they will pick up snakes with their hands; and when they drink deadly poison, it will not hurt them at all; <u>they will place their hands on sick people, and they will get well</u>***" Mark 16: 17 – 18. The question then is, do you believe in Him? If you do, that is what makes you a Christian, and that means you can perform healings and miracles.

While the Lord Jesus Christ was on earth, He performed many healings and miracles. When He sent out the twelve and the seventy-two, they came with a report of outstanding miracles. "***The seventy-two returned with joy and said, "Lord, even the demons submit to us in your name***" Luke 10: 17. Several other disciples and apostles performed great and astonishing healings and miracles. The Apostle Paul, Titus, Timothy, and several others performed miracles in their days.

"I tell you the truth, anyone who believes in me will do the same works I have done, and even greater works, because I am going to be with the Father" John 14: 12. To perform healings and miracles is by the Spirit of God in us. You are not the one performing the miracles per se. When you pray for someone or lay hands on a sick person to be healed, God only uses you as a channel to perform the miracle of healing. ***"And by the hands of the apostles were many signs and wonders wrought among the people; (and they were all with one accord in Solomon's porch"*** Acts 5:12.

Mr. Sele Cephas testifies...

"Sometime in June 2018, I led a group in my local church out for evangelism, soul-winning, and visitation. We got to a house where we met a woman who had something like boils all over her body – I mean from head to her toes, everywhere was covered up with these boil like infirmities. It was a pathetic sight to behold. But because my team members and I have been trained with the Word of God, we started preaching the Word of God to the woman, and soon, her husband came out from one of the rooms looking so sick with only God knows what. On seeing the man, I knew that the devil was out to destroy the entire family, and a wave of holy anger suddenly sprung up inside me.

After preaching for about ten minutes, I led the couples in the prayer of salvation, and they both got born again. I told them it was not God's will for them to remain in their conditions. I went further to show them a few Scriptures to prove to them that God was ready to heal them. I saw the excitement and faith on their faces. Then my team and I started praying for them, commanding the foul spirits of darkness that plagued them to come out of them. They fell under the power of the Holy Spirit and rolled on the floor.

After a while, they became still, and we helped them to their seats. They were filled with joy and faith by the time we were done praying. We invited them to church and ensured that they were present in the next service so that they could continue feeding on the Word of God. Within two months, there was no trace of any infirmities in their bodies. They went back to their job and businesses, for they were completely healed by the power of the Lord Jesus Christ."

Prayer

I believe in the power of God to heal even today. The Lord Jesus Christ is the same yesterday, today, and forever. What He did in Bible days, He is still doing through me in my world by the power of the Holy Spirit. Everywhere I go, I demonstrate the healing power of God, and miracles are wrought to the glory of God. Amen.

08 Sickness Is Not God's Will for You

God is not the author of sickness, and He does not use sickness to punish any of His children. So, sickness is not His will for you. There are Christian folks who believe that God can sometimes use sickness to humble or discipline Christians. This is not true because it has no foundation in the Word of God. The Bible says, "***How God anointed Jesus of Nazareth with the Holy Ghost and with power: who went about doing good, and healing all that were oppressed of the devil; for God was with him***" Acts 10: 38. If sickness is God's will or He uses it to humble His children, then God would not have anointed Jesus Christ to heal those who were oppressed by the devil.

If you believe that sickness is God's will or that He can use it to humble a Christian, why do you take drugs and visit the hospital to try to remove what you claimed that God put on you? If you are sick, pray to God for healing. The Lord Jesus Christ asked, "***Which of you if your son asks for bread, will give him a stone? Or if he asks for a fish, will give him a snake?***" Matthew 7: 9 – 10. You cannot be praying to God for divine health and healing when God gives you sickness. No, that is not God. "***So if you who are evil know how to give good gifts to your children, how much more will your Father in heaven give good things to those who ask Him***" Matthew 7: 11.

Inope Pius grew up in a Christian background that believes that some sicknesses are God's instruments to humble His children so that they will not be proud. So anytime he fell sick, he would cover himself under the duvet claiming that God has found some element of pride in him, and hence God put the sickness on him. He would even refuse to take prescribed drugs or go to the hospital.

Inope defends his believe with Scriptures such as Exodus 15: 26, "***Saying, "If you will diligently listen to the voice of the LORD your God, and do that which is right in his eyes, and give ear to his commandments and keep all his statutes, I will put none of the diseases on you that I put on the Egyptians, for I am the LORD, your healer.***" Or Deuteronomy 28: 27, "***The LORD will strike you with the boils of Egypt, and with tumors and scabs and itch, of which you cannot be healed***."

On December 15th, 2019, Inope suddenly fell ill to the point that he could not walk and could barely talk. He was rushed to a private hospital in his neighborhood where he spent his Christmas and the first few days of the New Year. When he recovered, the doctor of the hospital, a spirit-filled born again Christian, preached to him and expanded his understanding of the gospel. He told him that sickness is not God's will for His children. Today, Inope believes in divine health, healing, and the power of the Christian over the devil and sicknesses. Halleluiah!

Prayer

Dear Heavenly Father, I thank You for the knowledge and understanding that Your Word brought to me today. I understand that sickness or ill health is not your will for me. In the Name of the Lord Jesus Christ, I declare that I have authority over every sickness and infirmity; I live a sickness-free life by the power of the Holy Spirit. Amen.

09 Relationship between Forgiveness & Healing

There is a strong connection between forgiveness and healing. One day the Lord Jesus Christ asked the Pharisees and those around Him a question, "***Which is easier, to say, 'Your sins are forgiven you,' or to say, 'Rise and walk'?***" Luke 5: 23. That means the paralysis the young man who got healed had was connected to some form of sin he had committed. The young man needed his sin forgiven before he could be healed.

The Holy Spirit speaking through the Apostle James said, "***Therefore, confess your sins to one another and pray for one another, that you may be healed. The prayer of a righteous person has great power as it is working,***" James 5:16. Some Christians are afflicted with sicknesses because of the sins they committed. The Apostle Paul buttresses the fact that sin leads to sickness and death when he warned that the Holy Communion should not be taken unworthily. "***For anyone who eats and drinks without recognizing the body eats and drinks judgment on himself. That is why many of you are weak and sick and some have even died***" 1 Corinthians 11: 29-30. From what we discuss above, you can see that for some healing to take place, the folk that needs healing needs forgiveness first.

As a young teenager, Sammy was very close to his pastor. He slept over at his house and ran errands for him at times. Since they were close, Sammy had access to his pastor's bedroom and office in the church. He found himself stealing little sums of monies and other items. In his mind, his pastor would never notice because he was too busy and always had monies coming to him.

Sammy continued stealing for several years. He stole from his pastor and from the church monies. When his pastor would suspect, he found ways of distracting his attention. The Bible says, "***There is a way that appears to be right, but in the end it leads to death***" Proverbs 14: 12. Sammy thought he was a smart guy but never knew he was digging his own grave. He graduated from stealing from his pastor and church to stealing from his friends and family members.

When Sammy would show up in a place, something would go missing. It became a problem for his family and his friends. Even when he was caught in the act, he would try to get out of it. One day he was caught stealing a phone from another passenger in a public bus, and other passengers descended on him. They beat him so bad he lost consciousness and fell into a coma. When his pastor was called, he waited for him to regain consciousness before he prayed for him. The pastor forgave Sammy after he confessed how he had been stealing from the pastor, the church, and his loved ones. Sammy later testified that he saw someone walk out of him while his pastor prayed for him, and the urge to steal left him. Praise God!

Prayer

Precious Father, I thank You for the opportunity to receive forgiveness and healing. Lord, I ask for forgiveness for anything I probably might have done wrong knowingly or otherwise. I declare that by faith, I receive forgiveness and healing today, in Jesus' Name. Amen.

10 Walking in Divine Health

Is living in divine health really possible, you might ask? Yes, it is. In 3 John 1: 2, the Spirit of God said, "***Beloved, I wish above all things that you may prosper and be in health, even as your soul prospers.***" This is God's desire for every one of His children. God wants you to live a life without sicknesses, diseases, infirmities, or being subject to the depraving elements of this world. To perpetually live in divine health is the birthright of every child of God.

Living in divine health means no more running to the hospitals as a result of sickness. Remember that the Lord gave you power over the devil and sicknesses. "***And calling His twelve disciples to Him, Jesus gave them authority over unclean spirits, so that they could drive them out and heal every disease and sickness***" Matthew 10: 1. If the Lord gave you the power to heal every disease and sickness, you can as well direct that anointing on yourself to deal with any symptoms that might appear in your body.

To be able to live in divine health, you must maintain a life of consistent prayers and declarations of God's Word concerning your health. As many times in a day, proclaim Bible healing promises over your health. Live a hygienic lifestyle and exercise regularly.

Mr. Sele Cephas testifies of how he started living in divine health.

"Growing up as a young Christian, I was always in and out of the hospital for one form of sickness or the other, especially severe flu. I read and declared Bible healing promises and prayed to God for healing, but still fell sick. Many times, I wondered and asked myself questions as to why I still fall ill despite all the promises in the Bible.

As I began to study my Bible more and grew spiritually, I learned that living in divine health was my responsibility and not God's. So, I began to put the Word of God concerning health and healing to practice. When I felt any symptom, instead of rushing for the pills or to the hospital, I started declaring God's Word and praying fervently in the Spirit. I continued to pray in tongues until the symptoms disappeared. As I continued doing these, I noticed that I no longer had to make frequent visits to hospitals or use pills as I frequently did before. I told myself that if I have to visit any hospital, it is to go and pray for the sick to be healed. The Lord Jesus Christ said, "***And these signs will accompany those who believe: In My name they will drive out demons; they will speak in new tongues; they will pick up snakes with their hands; and when they drink deadly poison, it will not hurt them at all; they will place their hands on sick people, and they will get well***" Mark 16: 17 – 18.

For more than twenty-five years now, living in divine health has been my experience. I dared to believe and do exactly as the Word of God said. If I 'feel' any symptoms, instead of giving in to it, I will start praying in tongues and declaring God's Word over my body, especially in the area that I 'feel' the discomfort and soon, it will fade away.

Prayer

In the Name of the Lord Jesus Christ, I declare that living in divine health is continually my experience. My life is in Christ with God. I am conscious of the eternal life I have in Christ Jesus – the life that is impregnable by the devil and sicknesses. I declare wholeness in my health by the power of the Holy Spirit. I thank You, Dear Father. Amen.

11 The authority To Lay Hands on the Sick

Tremendous power is transmitted, and amazing things do happen by laying on of hands on the sick. You might look at your hands and conclude they are ordinary, but you are mistaken. The hands of a Christian are so anointed and full of tremendous power to heal the sick and even raise the dead. When you study the ministries of our Lord Jesus Christ, Apostles Peter, James, Philip, Paul, and several other disciples of Jesus in the Scriptures, you will find that they performed several miracles by the laying on of their hands. "***Then Jesus put out His hand and touched him, saying, "I am willing; be cleansed." Immediately his leprosy was cleansed***" Matthew 8: 3. "***By the hands of the apostles many signs and wonders were done among the people. They were all with one accord in Solomon's porch***" Acts 5: 12.

Understand that, as a born again Christian, your hands are not ordinary. You can lay those your hands on the sick, or even the dead and miracles will happen. The Lord Jesus Christ said of you, "***And these signs shall follow them that believe; In my name shall they cast out devils; they shall speak with new tongues; They shall take up serpents; and if they drink any deadly thing, it shall not hurt them; they shall lay hands on the sick, and they shall recover***" Mark 16: 17 – 18. Can you see that? He said you would lay hands on the sick and they will recover. Your duty is to lay hands, and through faith, the sick will draw from the anointing that is on you, and they will recover. So do not worry about the recovering, what you are required to do is to lay your hands.

In October 2018, Mrs. Omon Lucky woke around 5am feeling a bit shaky, but as a very busy woman, she waved it aside, thinking, 'Oh, I am a bit stressed up, and this must be due to lack of proper rest.' She went about her chores and left for work even though she was a little bit tired. As a teacher and a businesswoman, she would teach from 8am till 2pm. When the school closed, she would go to her shop to join her sales team and stay in the shop till about 7pm before going home to her family. Even on weekends, she would work around 10 to 12 hours per day.

On this fateful day, as they were winding down for the day, she became restless and started to feel weak. She sat down and tried to call one of her sales girls to help her, but words could not come out of her mouth. Suddenly, the right side of her body became numb. She fell on the floor, and that was when her sales girls knew something was wrong with her.

Mrs. Omon Lucky suffered a stroke and became incapacitated. Her husband and family took her to several hospitals and special healing homes, but her condition did not improve. According to her, in that almost lifeless state, all she could think about was how busy her life was, and although she was a Christian, serving God was a drag for her. She hardly went to church. She was always busy with her business. She felt very guilty and condemned. The devil kept telling her she was irredeemable and that God was very angry with her.

A year and three months into her condition, she made up her mind to die; the will to live vanished. However, God, in His infinite mercy, came to her rescue. She woke up one Sunday morning and asked her husband to take her to church. Though he was surprised, he obliged. At church, she was surprised at the love her pastor and members showed her. During the service, she made peace with God, and as if that was not enough, her pastor called her out for prayers. He laid hands on her to receive healing. That marked her recovery. Within the next few months, her health improved. Today Mrs. Omon Lucky is totally healed.

Prayer

I thank You, Precious Father, for the opportunity to demonstrate Your power and authority through the laying of my hands. I declare that on whomever, I lay my holy hands, healing, restoration, and health will be manifested in their bodies, in Jesus' Name. Amen.

12 Your Confessions & Your Health

By confessions, I mean the words you speak or say with your mouth. Understand that life and death are in the power of your tongue. You are either speaking life or death with your mouth. In other words, the words you speak are producing life, or they are draining the life out of you or what you speak about. "***Life and death are in the power of the tongue, and those who love it will eat its fruit***" Proverbs 18: 21.

As a Christian, be mindful of what you say, especially concerning your health. If you speak life, you will live. In the same vein, if you speak sickness, weakness, defeat, or death, that is what you will get in return. "***You are snared by the words of your mouth; you are taken by the words of your mouth,***" Proverbs 6: 2.

"***But I tell you that men will give an account on the Day of Judgment for every careless word they have spoken***" Matthew 12: 36. Understand that words do not die. Whatever you say as a joke, in anger or as ordinary words goes into your future with you. Your words are what produce your future. Whether you would live a healthy life or not is mostly dependent on your words. "***For by your words you will be acquitted and by your words you will be condemned***" Matthew 12: 37.

Sele Cephas testifies...

The environment one is raised in has a way of influencing one's words and lifestyle in general. I grew up in an environment where words or what you say were counted as nothing – mere words. I was used to hearing words like 'I am finished'; 'I am broke'; O' God, I am dead'; 'My head is a block'; 'Life is hard'; Everything is turning bad'; 'I am sick'; 'I am not well' etc. Naturally, these words and phrases became part of my everyday vocabulary. Little did I know that I was complicating my future! My words were forming like a cloud of rain waiting for the right time to empty itself on me and anything concerning me. "***If the clouds are full of rain, they empty themselves upon the earth; and if a tree falls to the south or the north, in the place where the tree falls, there it shall lie***" Ecclesiastes 11:3.

Though I was a Christian, my life was characterized by lack, constant struggle to make ends meet, frequent visits to the hospitals because of sickness, and one form of mishaps after another. My life, especially my health was far off from the reality of God's Word. I was experiencing constant pains instead of divine health.

One day, I decided to honor an invitation by my uncle to fellowship in his church. I went not expecting anything in particular. However, the conditions of my health and life, in general, were altered for good in that service. As I sat there, listening to the pastor preach a sermon that simply electrified me. He said words that at that time were outlandish. I heard him say 'You are in charge of your life;

'Your words will either make you or mar you'; Speak life to your job, business, family, marriage, etc.' 'There are no such thing as jokes in the realm of the spirit'; 'Your words are your life' and so on. These words hit my heart, and as if in a vision, I saw how the negative words I speak turned my life and health into obscurity.

So, I made up my mind that day that my words must reflect God's Word and minister grace. No matter what my condition was, I would speak God's Word concerning the situation instead of what or how I feel. Today, I can testify that my life goes in an upward and forward direction: no more sickness, lack, and confusion. Praise God!

Prayer

Lord God, I worship You for who You are. I thank You for teaching me today about the importance and the relationship between my words and my health. In the name of the Lord Jesus Christ, I declare I will always speak right. My words are seasoned with grace and healing by the power of the Holy Spirit. Amen.

13 How to Keep Your Healing

Healing is retainable. You can maintain your healing and remain in sound health perpetually. Do not be among the skeptical folks who do not believe in divine healing or health. The Word of God says that the Lord Jesus Christ went about doing good and healing all that were oppressed of the devil. "***How God anointed Jesus of Nazareth with the Holy Ghost and with power: who went about doing good, and healing all that were oppressed of the devil; for God was with Him***" Acts 10: 38.

Also, keeping your healing is not difficult. It is as simple as living the Word of God. If you have been sick and got healed, the one thing you must do to keep your healing is to live by the Word. The Lord Jesus Christ saw a man He had healed in the temple, and He told him to ensure he lived right, so something worse does not befall him. "***Afterward Jesus found him in the temple, and said to him, "See, you have been made well. Sin no more, lest a worse thing come upon you***" John 5: 14.

"***Be not deceived: evil communications corrupt good manners***" 1 Corinthians 15: 33. Another thing you must do to maintain your healing is to disassociate yourself from wrong people, places, and things you used to associate with that brought the sickness you were healed of. In John 5: 14, the Lord Jesus Christ said to the man He healed ***Sin no more, lest a worse thing come upon you***.

Proverbs 4: 20 – 22 says that the Word of God is life to those who find it and health to his whole body. Ensure that the Word of God is on your lips. Meditate on it day and night and ensure it never leaves your mouth. The Word of God in your mouth is your health. "***He sent His word and healed them, and delivered them from their destructions***" Psalm 107: 20.

Here is the testimony of Cutis Omoaho...

I got healed of Rheumatoid arthritis a few years back. In May 2019, I noticed the symptoms sneaking in again. I had suffered from this condition for over ten years. I made up my mind I will not tolerate or allow it into my body again. So, I did a quick check on myself and what I have been involved in lately. When I could not see or pinpoint any wrong from my end, I knew it was the devil that was introducing a counter-attack. What did I do? I went into fierce prayers, declared God's Word concerning my health, and exercised my faith by rebuking the pains.

*The Word of God says, "**Submit yourselves therefore to God. Resist the devil, and he will flee from you**" James 4: 7.* I prayed like never before for five days, declaring that I am healed and insisted that I remain healed. At first, it was as though nothing was happening, but on the fifth day, I noticed that all the symptoms were disappearing. I did not feel any pain or discomfort, and God has kept me in good health ever since. Halleluiah!

Prayer

In the Name of the Lord Jesus Christ, I declare that I live in perpetual health. No sickness, disease, or infirmity has the power to fasten itself on my body. I retain my healing and the divine health I have received as an inheritance in Christ Jesus by the power of the Holy Spirit. Amen.

14 He Is the God of Yesterday, Today & Tomorrow

Hebrews 13: 8 says, "***Jesus Christ is the same yesterday and today and forever.***" This means that the Lord Jesus would do for you today what He did for folks in Bible days. He will also do for those who ask of Him in the future. He heals today the same way He healed sick folks while He walked on this earth. He will also heal those who will be sick in the future.

He said to the disciples, "***Nevertheless, I tell you the truth: it is to your advantage that I go away, for if I do not go away, the Helper will not come to you. But if I go, I will send him to you***" John 16: 7. Today, it is that Helper, the Holy Spirit that heals us in the Name of the Lord Jesus Christ. The Holy Spirit answers to the Name of Jesus Christ. In other words, when you call the Name of Jesus today, it is the Holy Spirit that responds. "***But the Helper, the Holy Spirit, whom the Father will send in my Name…***" John 14: 26a.

You do not need to worry about your health or your future because they are secured in the Name of the Lord Jesus Christ. "***For you have died, and your life is hidden with Christ in God,***" Colossians 3: 3. Refuse to entertain any fear about your tomorrow. He is with you to keep you healthy. If He healed sick folks in Bible days and He is still healing people today, be rest assured that your future is safe with Him. Remember, He has authority over anything that is named in heaven, on earth, and under the earth. "***That at the name of Jesus every knee should bow, in heaven and on earth and under the earth***" Philippians 2: 10.

Mrs. Ruth Odia narrates her testimony...

Before I got born again and became a Christian, I used to laugh at Christians who claimed that they were healed of one ailment or the other. As far as I was concerned, both the preachers and those who claimed to have been healed were all deceivers. How can they claim that 'a carpenter's son" who lived thousands of years ago healed someone of diabetes, cancer, ulcer, blindness, paralysis, etc? They were all liars. I would conclude with anger.

In January 2017, I was involved in a ghastly motor accident. Not less than four people died. My left leg and arm were broken, and I was taken to a private orthopedic hospital. After spending a year and two months in the hospital, and after undergoing several surgeries, I was discharged to continue my recovery at home. As I started learning to walk again, I noticed that my left leg was shorter than the right leg by almost 5 inches. This made me feel bad as I had my left leg shoes padded to have a good balance as I began to walk again.

Though I was grateful that I did not lose my life, I still did not deem it necessary to give my life to Christ. God granted me an opportunity when a new neighbor invited me to her church on 31st December 2019, New Years' Eve Service. As I sat observing the proceedings in the service, I got a rude shock when the pastor called my name and described all that I went through because of the accident. He told me God loves me, and He shared my life to prove to me that He is the God of yesterday, today, and forever. The same way He performed miracles in the past, He will heal me to surprise me. I was speechless, to say the least.

The pastor led me to Christ, and afterward, stretched his hands towards my legs. He commanded the legs to be equal again. I fell under the power, and as I stood up, my legs were equal. Jesus! Jesus! Jesus! Those were the words I could shout. Today, I am healed, and my legs are perfectly equal. Glory to God!

Prayer

Dear Father, You are the God of yesterday, today, and tomorrow. What You did for one, You will do for another under the same circumstance. I thank You because You are still performing even today, the miracles you did in Bible days. I thank You, Lord, in Jesus' Name. Amen.

15 Confess Your Faults & Be Healed

By this, I mean that when you do something wrong and feel weighed down by guilt, approach your pastor, and confess to him or her. If you cannot readily reach your pastor, meet with a mature brother or sister, you can trust with your 'secrets.' "***Therefore, make it your habit to confess your sins to one another and to pray for one another, so that you may be healed. The prayer of a righteous person is powerful and effective***" James 5: 16.

For some Christian folks, even when they sincerely confess and ask God for forgiveness, they find it difficult to forgive themselves. Sometimes it could be the devil playing with their minds, and at other times, it could be as a result of deep ignorance of God's Word. The Word of God says, "***Even if our conscience condemns us, God is greater than our conscience, and He knows all things,***" 1 John 3: 20. Good knowledge of God's Word will save you from many troubles. When you sincerely ask God for forgiveness, He instantly forgives you. The guilt you might feel or accusations of men and the devil are inconsequential; they do not count at all. So when you approach your pastor or a fellow brother or sister, when you join the faith in prayers, it is to strengthen you and to heal you of any hurt or pain. This is why we are brethren – to help each out.

Patience John-Ero's Testimony

My name is Patience John-Ero; I grew up in a family where keeping malice or grudges was almost normal. My mum had grudges against my father that took place even before I was born. Though my dad was a free-spirit individual, when he became angry, he would remind you of things you did in the past that he was still upset about.

As I grew up and got married, this attitude of keeping malice became a challenge. My husband hardly remembers any wrong I did after a month or two. I admire this about him, and I prayerfully desired to cultivate this godly attitude, but it was a struggle for me. However, one day I summoned up courage and approached my pastor. I explained my background to him, and he took the time to share God's Word with me and afterward prayed with me. Instantly I felt a huge burden leave me and felt inner peace for the first time in my life. The love of God overwhelmed my heart, and I found I could easily forgive and love others. Praise God!

Prayer

Lord God, I thank You for the opportunity to confess our faults to one another, to pray for one another, and to receive healing. I declare that I receive healing from every hurt I suffered, in Jesus' Name. Amen.

CHAPTER 2

HEALING MIRACLE TESTIMONIES

TESTIMONY 01-God the Healer: From Impossible to a Beautiful Baby

"We are still attending follow-ups once a year, and the Neuro doctor is amazed and pleased whenever he sees him. Praise God! He's doing well in his school and being a witness for Christ."

Praise the Lord. God has given me a miracle child. It was my first pregnancy; I was so excited as all the mums who are pregnant for the first time. Despite having a problem of polycystic ovaries, I got pregnant a few months into our marriage. My husband and I were excited about going for a scan at 5months, wanting to know if it was a boy or a girl. I became little bit disappointed and worried when I looked at the face of the person doing the scan-who looked worried. My husband asked her if it was a boy or a girl. She said it's a boy but asked us to wait in the waiting room to discuss with the consultant as she had noticed a slight problem with the baby.

We both were praying and waiting in the room when the doctor entered. She told us that our boy had a very rare condition called DANDY WALKER VARIANT, in which a little part of his small brain (cerebellum) was missing. This could either lead him to be mentally retarded or his head could swell up with collection of fluid. They couldn't tell me how he was going to be at that time. Hence, they offered me to do an amniocentesis (taking some fluid from the womb by inserting a needle) to test it and abort the baby was incase the baby had the condition.

However, my husband and I refused to go for that test as we didn't want to abort the baby. With tears in my eyes, I told the doctor that we were going to pray. We informed our family members and church believers who prayed for us. Even some of the believers in the medical field thought that we are going to struggle with a mentally retarded baby, and it was not a wise decision to carry on with the pregnancy. Since that day, I have had to attend clinics every week. The doctors were scanning me and measuring the baby's head circumference every week, and they also did an MRI of his head when I was 7months pregnant.

When I was around 32 weeks pregnant, the doctors found that there was no blood supply from me to the baby anymore. So, they admitted me and said that they needed to take the baby out soon. I was given a steroid injection to mature the lungs of the baby, and at 34 weeks, they decided to do a caesarian section. They suspected that the baby would need to be admitted at Neonatal ICU, to get ventilator support...etc. Hence, they transferred me to another hospital where there were ICU beds available and carried out the operation and took him out. I was praying that he should cry straight away and should not need any ventilation. Tears ran down my cheeks when I heard him cry as they took him out, after a quick hug, they took him to the SCBU (special care baby unit). He was on oxygen for a couple of hours, IV infusion for a day, and NG tube feeding for another 2/3 days then he started taking breast milk. He was only 1.25kgs. They discharged him after 3 weeks. The doctors continued to review and measure his head for a few years. They then did an MRI when he was about 7 years old, which still shows that the condition is still there, but he's growing to be a normal child. We are still attending follow-ups once a year, and the Neuro doctor is amazed and pleased whenever he sees him. Praise God! He's doing well in his school and being a witness for Christ.

TESTIMONY 02 – God Held My Child In My Weak Placenta.

"I was so happy that all things worked for good and all my fear disappeared. As God promised in Romans: 8:28 "all things God works for good ". God helped me to give birth to a Healthy baby boy. None of my health issues like thyroid or any other illness affected my child. We christened our baby as "JOEN" which means "Gift from GOD", Yeah truly he is a Gift from God.!!"

"And we know that in all things God works for the good of those who love him, who have been called according to his purpose" (Rom:8:28).

I'm going to share my testimony with you, which I believe will give hope to the hopeless. By the purest Grace of Lord Jesus, I conceived after a month of entering my marriage, and during my pregnancy, I had many health issues like thyroid and so on. I used to lay my hands on my abdomen every day and pray to God for the child, its growth, and especially for normal delivery.

Before the due date of my delivery, because of the leaking membrane, I was admitted in the hospital for delivery. I didn't have any delivery pain even-though I was induced to give birth as I was in great pain. Doctors waited from morning till noon, but the position of my baby's head didn't turn up in the right position for normal delivery, and it was immobile. So the Doctor informed us that I had less chance for normal delivery, and I had to go for a C-section to save the baby.

I was devastated by the news, and my blood pressure level went high because I am the kind of person who easily gets scared even when I go for vaccination. Fear filled me up, but I remembered a verse that comforted me in the labour room ***"My presence will go with you, and I will give you rest" (Exodus 33:14)***. I was pondering on the word and prayed to God in the operation theatre. Then I saw this verse on a plaque ***"The Lord is my shepherd, I shall not be in want" (Psalms: 23-1).***

I gave birth to a baby boy through C- section, and during the surgery, my Doctor exclaimed, *"Really, God's grace is with you because your placenta is very weak and feeble, and it has multiple cysts too".* She continued saying that a child can't grow in a thin bag. In addition to that, she explained that there are only two possibilities that could have happened, either the child would have been aborted at an early stage of pregnancy, or it could not end up being abnormal.

I was confused initially because I did not understand why God allowed me to go through a C-section, but after hearing my Doctor's words, I was so happy that all things worked for good, and all my fear disappeared. As God promised in Romans: 8:28, "all things work for the good". God helped me to give birth to a healthy baby boy. None of my health issues like thyroid or any other illness affected my child.

TESTIMONY 03 – God healed me completely and prevented the scheduled operation for removing the limbs due to Peripheral Artery Disease.

"When the surgeon went to inspect the leg, he could not figure out which leg needed to be amputated. The chart said one thing, but that is not what he was seeing. Her leg had been completely healed, and although the surgeon had no explanation, my friend certainly knew who had healed her. She then spent the next thirty minutes explaining to the doctor it was God who healed her leg.

God still heals! Praise God!"

I was talking to a friend, who happens to be elderly, about a prayer request she had regarding one of her legs. She had developed Peripheral Artery Disease (PAD) due to her type 2 diabetes. PAD causes blood vessels to narrow and reduces blood flow to the legs and feet, thus causing one to develop sores and, eventually, the loss of limbs. Her sickness was well advanced, and by the time I was talking to her, the diagnosis was completed, and the surgery date was just a few days away. I knew things were bad because I could see the bandages on her leg needed to be redressed due to the open sores. She had advanced so far into the sickness that the removal of the leg was the only option, or so everyone thought.

I got down on my knees next to her and put my hands on her bandaged leg. I was a little worried that I was going to hurt her, but I knew the prayer would be short, and the prayer would be worth any discomfort she was temporarily in. I prayed, acknowledging Jesus as the ultimate healer and asked him to take away any discomfort or pain she was in. I prayed for the doctors and nurses who were going to take care of her during and after the operation. I prayed for the surgery itself and that Jesus would reassure her of his presence during the surgery. And then I felt a boldness to pray for total healing of the leg. I mentioned that God raised Jesus from the dead, and that he healed so many people throughout his ministry here on earth and that he still heals people today. I ended the prayer and gave my friend a hug and said I would check up on her after the surgery.

A few days later, I got a call from my friend. She had seen the doctor, and she wanted to tell me all about it. I asked her about the surgery and thought it was a little strange she would be calling me. I had planned to visit her in the hospital, but the operation never happened. She was telling me this with tears in her eyes. Although I could not physically see her because we were on the phone, I could definitely tell there were tears in her eyes because of the way she was sniffling over the phone. These were tears of joy. She told me she went to the hospital, and during the pre-opt, when the surgeon went to inspect the leg, he could not figure out which leg needed to be amputated!. The chart said one thing, but that is not what he was seeing. Her leg had been completely healed, and although the surgeon had no explanation, my friend certainly knew who had healed her. She then spent the next thirty minutes explaining to the doctor it was God who healed her leg.

God still heals! Praise God!

Testimony 04 – My Healer protected me after a Major Accident and made me walk again.

God's words gave me hope and strength to walk. I realized one thing after the incident, and that was, "Trusting God in light is nothing but to trust him while our skies are grey, that is faith" With faith, we can move the mountains, and that worked out for me. If God says yes, then nobody can say no. Trust God, don't give up and have faith. He is the healer, and faith can move mountains.

I am Glady, a physiotherapist by profession. I am here to witness the miracle which God has done for me. Even though I was born in a Christian family, I was always cynical and lacked faith in God, until I got into an accident on May 3rd, 2019, which completely changed my life. A car dashed my bike and dragged me up about 50 meters away. No one noticed that I was thrown away for a while.

When they did, they ran and came to lift me up. My hair was under the car wheel, and I was unable to get up. I was taken to the nearest hospital. Everyone thought that I was dying because I was unconscious and totally unaware of what was happening around me. I still remember pleading with God to save me in my subconscious, and I felt the touch of God. My body gets shivers even now when typing about the presence of God's power, which I felt that day. Though I was unconscious for more than 2 hours, I was aware that God had healed me and protected me from death in my subconscious.

When I regained consciousness, do you know what I did? I shouted and just said, "Thank you, Jesus". I knew that by His stripes, I was healed and true to His promise. His stripes healed me. Despite being dragged by a car on the road, I sustained only minor wound s and a deep cut on my ankle. The wounds and the cut were nothing compared to the seriousness of the accident. My whole family was so worried, but by the grace of God, I started walking on the 10th day after four dressings, I cried while walking, but God's words gave me hope and strength to walk. I realized one thing after the incident, and that was: "Trusting God in light is nothing but to trust him while our skies are grey, that is faith."

With faith, we can move the mountains, and that worked out for me. If God says yes, then nobody can say no. Trust God, don't give up and have faith. He is the healer, and faith can move mountains.

Testimony 05 – God miraculously healed my broken pelvis.

"Friday morning, I woke up. Humm—not in much pain, and I was able to stand on my feet much longer. By Sunday (not kidding), I was throwing horseshoes with my boy, pain-free, I loaded and unloaded 3 moving trucks, and I've been on the go ever since. I thank my Lord Jesus Christ and His faithful servant Bruce Carlson for the miracle of healing."

Three days before Thanksgiving, my daughter and I decided to go horse riding. While warming up the horses in our arena, I was thrown by my young horse. I knew it was serious; I couldn't move, and the pain was excruciating. After X-rays and CAT scan, they discovered I had separated my pelvis and had internal injuries. After a few days in the ICU and some time in recovery, I was back home and on the mend. With the help of physiotherapy, I was back on my feet in just six weeks. All seemed to be going well, but the pain in my hips began to increase. Around three months after the accident, I could barely walk, and the pain was unbearable. More X-rays and an MRI showed that my pelvis had become "unstable" & was separating again, putting pressure on my hip joints. My orthopedic surgeon recommendation was a plan that involved metal plates, screws, along with the risk that it might not relieve the pain, and it could break as I take part in various activities. None of the options sounded good, and so, depressed and feeling defeated, my wife and I began to pray.

God had a better plan that I just didn't know at that time. My friend James came over to shoe my horse and realized how painful it was for me to stand and keep the horse calm. He mentioned that his friend Bruce Carlson was in town and that he had prayed for people like me, and God healed them. He wondered if I would be interested in visiting him so that we can see what God might do.

James and I met him at his ranch. I shared with Bruce what had happened and how my pelvis actually shifted and separated as I tried to move, and how the pain was so bad that I could barely walk, sit, or stand. He asked me to have a seat right there in a straight back chair. Bruce held the heels of my feet in his hands, the three of us could all see that the right one was an inch or so shorter than the other. We could see that the pelvis was out of alignment. Bruce began to pray, taking God's word as true, and trusting Christ would do as He promised. As He prayed, I saw with my own eyes the right heel go out and pass the other, then it aligned perfectly as the left. "God is putting your pelvis back in alignment," Bruce explained. He asked me to stand as he prayed while laying his hands on my hips, again believing in Christ and His word for the power of healing. I could actually feel someone squeezing the SI joints together. When Bruce had finished praying for me, I could tell that something was different. Still, in pain, I went home - that was Thursday. Friday morning, I woke up. Humm—not as much pain, and I was able to stand on my feet much longer. By Sunday (not kidding), I was throwing horseshoes with my boy pain-free. I loaded and unloaded

3 moving trucks, and I've been on the go ever since. I thank my Lord Jesus Christ and His faithful servant Bruce Carlson for the miracle of healing.

Testimony 06 – God gifted me, twins, from a weak body

"I was in shock and jumped with excitement as I told my husband how great God is. It's been more than 7 years now that I was healed, and never did I have that pain again. That verse 'Be still and know that I am God' always reminds me of those days of anxiety and great pain whenever I read it."

I always believed God blessed me with a healthy and robust body compared with other women. But when I was around 28years old, I took a life insurance policy that required a medical examination. The insurance agent came back to me with devastating news...I was told that I had a heart attack before and that my ECG readings were abnormal.

To confirm this, I was taken to 3 more doctors, who also said the same. My menstrual cycle was also irregular because of PCOD. I refused to believe these reports and prayed over them.

Later, when I got married, my blood pressure shot up a couple of times. I was told by the doctor that it might be difficult to conceive with my condition. I was very depressed and anxious about all this. We went to many doctors for the blood pressure examination. Finally, we met with a great chief doctor who worked in a well-reputed hospital that specialized in heart issues. He said I had no problems except for the PCOD, which shoots up my pressure when there's a hormonal change.

Meanwhile, I confessed all my wrong ways, and I plead for forgiveness to my God.

Finally, I received a verse as a response: Isaiah 54: 7 - 9

"For a brief moment, I forsook you but with great compassion I will gather you. In overflowing wrath for a moment, I hid my face from you, but with everlasting love I will have compassion on you, says the Lord, your Redeemer"

Later I gave birth to twin boys, which I always see as a sign of God's forgiveness. It was a great joy that can't be put in words. My husband prayed for my PCOD issues every day in family prayer for 18 months, and we never went to any doctor for treatment. It just got healed without my knowledge, and I haven't had any issues for the past 7-8 years now. My first delivery was a bundle of joy from God but brought a lot of tough moments. One of them was my stomach ulcer.

My health became very poor after delivery, and the stomach ulcers left me feeling helpless. It was a huge pain day and night, whether I ate or not or whatever I ate. I didn't even have time to visit a doctor or think through a way to get healed as I had to look after 2 premature babies.

Many times I used to hold my stomach tight and slide down because of the pain. But it never struck my mind that I had to pray for the pain, and I started to accept it. This went on for close to 2 years. I got pregnant with our third child, and as I got to the last trimester of my second pregnancy, I became very anxious about how I would raise up the third child with my health condition, and yet the elder ones were hardly 2 years old. That time I got a verse from God which I held on to. ***Psalm 46:10 "Be still and know that I am God."***

I was struggling with pain one day, and yet the delivery date was near. So I cried to the Lord, "God, I can't imagine managing three kids with this enormous pain. I just can't handle it anymore. So please heal me the day my child is born" ...I seriously didn't know why I prayed that way. I was still in pain every day and night 24hours and even forgot what I prayed.

After 3-4 weeks, I was in the operation theatre preparing for the delivery but still experienced the same excruciating pain in my stomach. When I bore a daughter, I totally forgot about everything, and my eyes were on her all the time. God filled me up with joy that it took me five days to realize that the ulcer pain was not there from the moment I bore my child. I was in shock and jumped with excitement as I told my husband how great God is. It's been more than 7 years now that I was healed, and never have I had that pain again. That verse 'Be still and know that I am God' always reminds me of those days of anxiety and great pain whenever I read it."

Testimony 07 – My Cancer Was Healed Completely

"On 12 December 2011, God gave me an excellent report. The X-ray films showed the lungs were all cleared except for the scarring in the right upper lobe. The blood tests of the liver, kidneys and everything else had returned to normal. Praise God for God's healing miracle."

I thank God for His mercies and grace for His healing of my stage four lung cancer. In March 2011, I went for a routine checkup, and the X-ray showed a shadow in my right upper lobe.

As I sat in front of the doctor, all kinds of questions raced through my mind. A biopsy and scan revealed more bad news. The shadow turned out to be a 2.2×2.3×2.8 nodule on the right upper lobe with additional ground-glass opacity nodular lesions in the left upper and right lower lobe. It was confirmed that I had advanced multi-focal cancer involving both lungs.

As the news sank in, I began to be filled with fears and anxieties. I felt that I did not have much time left. I started to clear and dispose of my stuff. I cried out to our Lord for help, and He heard my cries, for He said to me in Psalms 118:17, ***"I shall not die but live to declare the works of the Lord."***

I was put on chemotherapy, and I began to suffer the side effects.

By God's grace, on 30 October 2011, I stepped into Cornerstone Community Church. I believe God was leading me as I was seeking Him. The worship songs and messages gave me comfort and assurance that Jesus is Lord and has power over heaven and earth. Nothing is too hard or impossible for Him. I claimed His Word in Jeremiah 33:3, ***"Call unto me, and I will answer you and show you great and mighty things which thou knowest not."***

On 27 November 2011, after the service, I responded to the altar call by Mattheus Van der Steen. Praise the Lord, He led me to step forward. During the anointing prayer, I had excruciating pain in my head, and as a sister continued to pray, the pain went away.

I thank God for sending Martin, Soh Hian, and Francis to visit, pray, and encourage me through that difficult period. Their belief and confidence in our Lord Jesus, who heals, gave me peace. After each service, I stepped forward for the healing prayer. Praise the Lord; two weeks before my monthly review, I had the peace that I was already healed because He is my Jehovah-Rapha.

On 12 December 2011, God gave me an excellent report. The X-ray films showed the lungs were all cleared except for the scarring in the right upper lobe. The blood tests of the liver, kidneys and everything else had returned to normal. Praise God for God's healing miracle.

Testimony 08: Healed from Cancer Completely

"It is clear that the Lord healed Jim of this very aggressive cancer. We give Him glory."

We rejoice with the family that Jim did indeed experience the goodness of the Lord and receive his healing on that June morning as everyone was leaving."

One Sunday morning in 2019, at the end of our Forerunner Christian Fellowship morning services, one small family group remained at the front where people had been receiving prayers. They were huddled around a man in his fifties, and looked concerned, hoping for a tangible touch of the goodness of the Lord. As they were preparing to leave, two of our pastors were asked to pray for the man. They prayed. The family thanked them. Names were exchanged, and everyone went their separate ways. And that is sometimes all that happens when we pray for and minister to people. We pray the promises of God and are left-leaning into the goodness and sovereignty of the Lord, not knowing what happened to the one whom we prayed for.

Four weeks later, we received an email from the family, as follows:

"In June this year, we were in Kansas City for a wedding and decided to attend Forerunner Christian Fellowship after spending half an hour in the prayer room. At the end of the service, my brother decided to go forward for prayer. He has been battling stage IV cancer. A couple of the church elders prayed for him.

The following is an email from one of my brother's doctors.

"Jim* has had stage IV cancer. It had metastasized, causing four masses in his brain. It had also metastasized to his lymphatic system and to the lining around the lung. On Tuesday, June 24, two days after he was prayed for, Jim had a scan and was pronounced completely cancer-free. This is impossible and can only happen with medical treatment. It is clear that the Lord healed Jim of this very aggressive cancer. We give Him glory."

We rejoice with the family that Jim did indeed experience the goodness of the Lord and receive his healing on that June morning as everyone was leaving.

"Now to Him who is able to do exceedingly abundantly above all that we ask or think, according to the power that works in us, to Him be glory in the church by Christ Jesus to all generations, forever and ever. Amen." (Ephesians 3:20–21).

Testimony 09 –Tumour, no more!

"I noticed after about a month, that the tumor had become smaller. I wasn't surprised, because I knew I was healed. Within six months, it was gone entirely. God is the real healer, and he heals even now. Trust him. "

Mike didn't pay much attention to the small sore on his chest. It started out as a minor annoyance—an itch that wouldn't go away. But after a year, he decided to get it checked out.

"When I first walked into the doctor's office, I wasn't afraid, just curious as to what was causing this sore," remembers Mike. "But the doctor took one look, and the next thing I knew is that he had me scheduled for emergency surgery." Mike did not understand the diagnosis at first—malignant neoplasm—so he asked his wife to research it while he returned to work.

His wife called him at work with the layman's terminology: "malignant skin tumor." A spirit of fear instantly gripped him. "My pastor told me not to do anything in fear, so I canceled my surgery until I could get peace," says Mike. Mike's doctor called him back immediately, warning him of the seriousness of his condition and let him know that if he refused surgery, he would stop being his doctor.

This drove Mike further into fear, but deep down, he knew God could heal him. He turned to God's Word. He searched the Word looking for things he could do to get God to move on his behalf. "I was taught that everything God did for me was based on my performance. As soon as I thought I'd finally measured up, the bar got raised, and I had to do more."

As Mike struggled with confusion and discouragement, the lesion changed into a tumor and began growing at an alarming rate. "I was told that it could metastasize throughout my body, and that's what began happening," says Mike. "For the next five years, it clung to me and sucked the life right out of me. I grew so weak, I had to quit my job. I give up the business I started, and at one point, even hold my head up to eat."

I started praying and believing in the word of God. Our family and all prayer partners prayed. Initially, there was no improvement, but we never gave up our prayers. Prayers started changing things. Faith can change any situation, and "I noticed after about a month, the tumor got smaller. I wasn't surprised, because I knew I was healed. Within six months, it was completely gone. God is the real healer, and he heals even now. Trust him."

Testimony 10 -God Protected and Healed Me Miraculously from A major Heart Attack

"Our financial situation was not good, and we could not afford to pay, but God opened his resources for us. We got the money for the surgery from various people by grace. God not only safeguarded me from the verge of death but also helped in getting proper treatment and provided the funds to pay for the operation. God is so good, and I will always trust Him fully at all times."

Psalm 46 says, **"God is our refuge and strength, a very present help in trouble."** This verse came true in my life on October 4th of 2019. I had been feeling tired in my body for a couple of days, and on that day, I became totally sick. We thought that it was giddiness or some sort of tiredness due to my being diabetic.

We went to a specialist for a consultation, but he was not available on that day. I started sweating so much, and I could feel that I was about to collapse.

My husband noticed that I was about to collapse. We were stuck, we didn't know how to proceed and which doctor to consult. So we rushed to a nearby hospital. Doctors examined and took ECHO and ECG, and they said everything was fine. "The tiredness might be because of the low sugar," the doctor concluded. We were happy with the results, so we went back home. However, the pain and the tiredness prevented me from falling asleep even for a single minute in the night. I was saying aloud all the promises which God has promised, and I kept the faith that my life is in His hand, and no enemy can take it away without His will.

The next day the same situation continued, and my son asked to consult some other hospital. He then made an appointment with a specialist, and we explained everything that happened the previous day. After looking at the ECG report, he confirmed that the ECG has not been appropriately taken and asked to take another ECG there and then. After that, the specialist told me that I had a massive heart attack the previous day. It was the grace of God that saved me that day. I was in the hospital immediately as they wanted to monitor my condition. The doctor said that due to the massive attack which had happened the previous day, there were more chances of cardiac arrest.

I was monitored for 2 days and was asked to go for surgery. Our financial situation was not good, and we could not afford to pay, but God opened his resources for us. We got the money for the surgery from various people by grace. God not only safeguarded me from the verge of death but also helped in getting proper treatment and provided the funds to pay for the operation. God is so good, and I will always trust Him fully at all times.

PART IV

Seven Poems on Healing Miracles

1. There is absolutely NO reason why Miracles in the Modern Day shouldn't be as normal as it was when Christ was on earth 2000 years ago—Christ performed miracles wherever He went.

Same Miracles

Like the rising of the sun
Same as the fall of night
One with the brilliance of gold
Where change is not mentioned
No matter the flow of sand in the hourglass.

Same as the creation of humanity
Identical like the elements of life itself
For none has changed from day one
As the creator remained unique
So His creation.

Same yesterday, same today
So is His tomorrow
As far as He remains the same
His miracles are His likes
For nothing has never remained the same.

2. You should see God as the source of miracles

The Fountain of Miracles

Like a river oozing from the fountain
With purity as that of its source
Where neither a molecule differs
Nor a droplet that of kerosene
From Him, they come, like Him, they are.

As the ewe brings forth the lamb
A chick from a hen it comes
While the cob is born from a lioness
And the sow gives life to a piglet
So do miracles from God they come.

As no apple tree bears a mango
So do avocados not fall from orange trees
While cures come from doctors
Healing comes from the creator
So do miracles.

3. You should believe in the God of miracles.

The God of Miracles

Looking up to the skies
Watching the stars aligned in the cosmos
Where distance has no measure
Light rays having no end
Believing in the creator remains the way.

Regaining health within the eyes twinkle
The mentally deranged thinking straight
The deformed becoming whole
Those without breath revived
All by Him above.

Living a new day with all confidence
Embracing it with a full agenda
And laying plans in all certainty
Who clears off the uncertainty
But He who made life possible.

4. You should be convinced that your life is made for miracles.

Made for Miracles

A drawing on the artist's board
Where either the eraser or highlighter is awaited
A spanner in the mechanic's hands
Meant either to tie or untie
Mere creatures for miracles we are.

A cup of water to wet the throat
A bowl of wheat to chase the hunger
A piece of cloth to hide nudity
A staff to accompany the lame
Mere creatures for miracle we are.

The writer's ink
Which writes nothing but the writer's mind
The driver's wheel
Which turns to wherever directed
Mere creatures for God's miracles we are.

5. Stop looking at symptoms & circumstances that cause concern, pain, or suffering.

The Viewer's Angle

Eyes wide open to gaze the nature
Filled with beauty and the ugly alike
Who sees the ugly but is he who looks at it
For beauty or ugly lays in the viewer's eyes.

Pain and enjoyment cooking in the same pot
Where the chief serves at the client's command
Feeding can only be on voluntary quest
For pain or enjoyment are always on the menu.

In the heart of the summer noon
Where the sun shines bright overhead
Who dares call it midnight
But he who keeps his eyes closed
As life is seen only at the viewer's angle.

6. See all problems as opportunities for imminent miracles.

The Positivity of Negation

Like a stone to the concrete builder
Not to a glassmaker
Like a stone to a drowning swimmer
Not to a ship docker
But problems remain opportunities.

Like a fallen child learning to grasp
Like a beaten warrior gaining experience
Like an electrician learning to tie the rope
Like a rider learning to wear a helmet
For if there be no problems, miracles remain myths.

Without darkness
Never will the light be so appreciated
Without pain
Enjoyment will not be this cherished
Without blindness
Never will vision be the light of the soul
For only in problems can miracles show themselves.

7. Believe and say to yourself every day, "My Lord, I believe that you are the God of Miracles and that you have created me to see every challenge and every problem I face as an opportunity for a miracle that you are ready, willing and about to perform."

I Believe

Gifted at every wake
Filled with breath and blessed with bread
Endowed in His image and likeness
Dark and long the night was
Yet who brought the dawn but Him.

Heart racing like a shuttle
Bleeding in the life of pain
Braving the fright of challenge
And sleep-walking when in peace
Yet none sets the pace but Him.

Turning the pain to gain
Pulling the timid hearts to fame
Trading the problems to opportunities

Filling the thirst with a fountain
For Miracle remains His first name.

PART V

ABOUT THE AUTHOR
&
ALL BOOKS PUBLISHED
BY AUTHOR OF THIS BOOK

ABOUT THE AUTHOR

Selva Sugunendran built a successful U.K. based IT company. After twenty-five years at the helm, he sold his business to pursue a greater, more meaningful passion: helping others to find success. Since leaving his company, he has inspired countless people from all walks of life to recognize their strengths and find their paths to success in life and business. He's also expanded his reach by penning multiple books, chapters, and guest posts that spread his proven ideology and methods for individual growth for people of all ages.

Named an Expert Platinum Author, his work has afforded him opportunities to meet and work with people of all ages and learn first-hand what they need to achieve optimal success. One such area that captured his interest is the plight of those living with dementia. Since obtaining a University Diploma on Dementia Prevention and some considerable research, he recently published his 5th book on Alzheimer's/dementia, titled, "***You Can Beat Alzheimer's—Let Me Show You How***" to give hope and clear steps for the prevention of this dreaded disease, using his unique **S.E.L.V.A.S Protocol**. It offers insight in an easy-to-digest format that will help anyone determined to prevent the onset of Alzheimer's. As well as to those who have just been diagnosed with the disease to understand its nuances and know what signs to look for and what questions to ask health care providers and how to delay its progress and in some cases even reverse it.

A year ago, he realized that all his books were based on *scientific analysis* and *medical research. A*s a devout Christian, he decided to research and write his latest book, based on the *healing promises* taken from the Holy Bible. This new book, ***"Empowering Healing & Hope Through Faith,"*** is the result of his work.

This book became a #1 Best Seller, and many people felt truly blessed. However, it soon became clear that there were some people, including church members who seemed to feel that the miracles that were "normal" when Christ was on earth don't happen as much in the modern world.

In this book, he has expanded on 7 key facts about modern-day healing miracles to prove beyond doubt that today miracles can be normal as they were before for those who seek them through Christ Jesus.

He has included several modern-day healing testimonies as well as positive affirmations supported by the word of God to build the faith so that readers can experience the miracles that people enjoyed when Christ was on earth.

This book should complement his previous book titled,

"Empowering Healing & Hope Through Faith"

When not writing or researching, Selva can be found exploring new ways to lift others and help them live the life of their dreams.

BOOKS ON CREATION & EVOLUTION

BOOKS ON WELLNESS & HEALTH

10

11

12

13

14

BOOKS ON ALZHEIMER'S & DEMENTIA

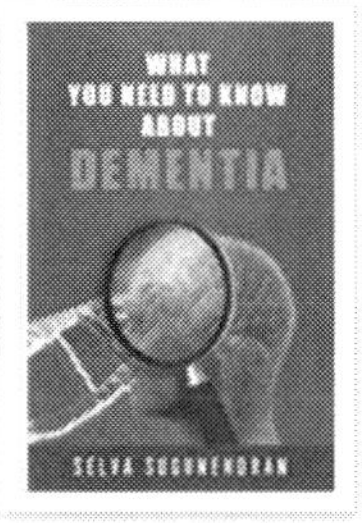

BOOKS ON SUCCESS

15

16

17

BOOKS ON HEALING & MIRACLES

APPENDICES

1. WEBSITE LINKS

http://BlessMeLord.com

http://HealMeLord.today

http://DementiaAdvice.care

http://ModernDayMiracles.com

http://PreventDelayReverseAlzheimers.com

http://CreationEvolutionAndScience.com

http://ModernDayHealingMiracles.com

ALL MY BOOKS: https://geni.us/betterlife

AUTHOR CENTRE: https://geni.us/betterhealth

THE BOOK ON HEALING: https://geni.us/HealingHopeFaith

THE BOOK ON MIRACLES: TBA

2. CONTACT LINKS:

The Author (Email): Info@BlessMeLord.com

Printed in Poland
by Amazon Fulfillment
Poland Sp. z o.o., Wrocław

63356283R00153